The Way We Were

The Way We Were

Carol A Healy

Published by Silver Star Books

silverstarbooksuk@yahoo.com

ISBN:
978-1-80227-817-0 (eBook)
978-1-80227-816-3 (paperback)

My book is dedicated to my amazing, wonderful son John, my brilliant respiratory consultant Dr Anjani Prasad, and the wonderful medical and ancillary team who looked after me with such dedication last year between the 24th March and the 22nd April 2021. They often saw me writing every day and asked if they could be included, so with gratitude for their exceptional care, I promised I would remember them. Next, I must not forget dear Gus at Chess Pharmacy in Chesham, Buckinghamshire, for whom nothing is too much trouble. And finally, my thanks must go to Debbie Poulsom for listening to the reading of the text.

CONTENTS

PREFACE

Over the years, friends and acquaintances, along with my son more recently, have repeatedly encouraged me to write a book, as the clichéd expression goes, a thought which I have often considered fairly seriously because they appreciate listening to my adventures, exploits, and reminiscences with real enthusiasm. Building on such a firm foundation, in addition to having the publication of several short pieces behind me, there is a rather pressing and meaningful message needing to be passed on to the readers as we enter yet another phase of uncertainty about our future in this country and any possibility of a return to life as we know it, one that resonates with my childhood experiences in the Lake District during the Second World War. Even though it was a long time ago, the memories have come flooding back so clearly and in plentiful quantity. Spontaneous recall of such a variety to my mind has suggested that my story should be told in sections rather than using the traditional chapter format for the sake of creating a more atmospheric, memorable, and poignant account with greater appeal and impact.

INTRODUCTION

The profound and long-lasting effects that the Coronavirus pandemic has been having on the population of this country since March 2020 have reminded me powerfully of how it was in my own early years, having been born in 1935, and have made me think that people now might be interested to read about what life was like for people then to live through very dark times and manage to come out the other side, not unscathed but triumphant. What it was like to be facing another major war hopelessly and terrifyingly unprepared in a world with little communication as we expect now and with primitive living conditions. For example, there was no NHS or health care provision worthy of mentioning, interrupted education with schools closed because of bombings, or people being evacuated to safer places for years. Besides the latter, there were shortages of food and clothes – rationing lasted until 1950, particularly fuel like petrol. And, as if this situation was not bad enough, people of the 20th century of my parents' generation and grandparents had endured the First World War 1914–1918, the post-war pandemic of Spanish Flu 1919, the Great Depression of 1929 with the sudden shutdown of businesses and rock bottom opportunities before the lead up to World War II came hard on its heels.

There have been adverse reactions to the restrictions imposed by COVID-19, and the length of the deprivation – is understandable, but it has not been a case of lurching from one long disaster to another in fairly quick succession or having the duration of six years of uncertainty dropped on us as I and my contemporaries remember.

SETTING THE SCENE

Of great importance is reflecting on two truly brilliant and very special "Rare Birds." Unsung heroes to me, they came from a shaky start and a troubled beginning, respectively.

Harry McEvoy, my father, was born in Bradford, Yorkshire, on 16th August 1902 and typified the relentless determination and optimism needed to survive the blow after blow events that life dealt him, his family, and so many others in this country during the first half of the 20th century. So mesmerised were people who knew my father's resilience and ability to survive adversity that after he died on November 3rd, 1984, I received calls from his many friends, work associates, and former employees saying they had heard rumours of his death but did not believe it could be true. It was hard, even for me, his daughter, to convince them that, sadly, it was really the end of the line for him, and the funeral had already taken place.

Having narrowly missed being called up into the forces in the First World War – my father was 16 when the war ended in 1918 – he was helping as an orderly at St Luke's Hospital as a war effort pushing trolleys, etc. He left school (Bradford Grammar School) and started his career as a cloth salesman, which he loved. He was instantly very successful and was able to buy a house, marry my mother Hilda on 23rd February 1926 when he was twenty-three, and take her for a honeymoon on a Mediterranean Cruise!

In 1928 my sister Patricia was born.

Life seemed to be going smoothly, and then came the Great Depression in 1929, which lasted until 1933. My maternal grandfather, who had become very prosperous and owned a woollen mill in Bradford and several shops in the city, lost everything as businesses large and small went bankrupt. He had had a spacious house in Ash Grove, Bradford, with a sizeable garden in which my mother remembered as a child was a de-commissioned tramcar her father had bought for her to play in and a retired racehorse called Prince. My father told me how soul-destroying it became for him when his loyal customers were closing down everywhere and selling anything became impossible. It was then that one of grandad's wealthy business associates said that my father's only option was to go to America as an immigrant, and he kindly gave him the money to pay the fare to make the journey.

With a heavy heart, he set sail for New York in 1931 on the S.S. Berengaria to try and earn enough money to send home for my mother and sister. He used to tell me that his homesickness was like a terrible illness and almost overwhelming, but somehow, he earned money playing the piano in the Y.M.C.A working shifts in department stores, and he paid for his business degree at Columbia University in New York. Americans were very kind. He made friends and was attracted to their way of life even though times were incredibly tough in the States, too, with Prohibition.

Interestingly, I think my father was exceedingly tall at 6ft 3ins from his Norwegian grandfather, and his very long arms meant English tailoring did not fit him, but he could always buy off the peg suits in America. Having graduated with the degree he needed and too poor to buy a newspaper, he went to the Grand Central Library in New York to look at the Situations Vacant pages in newspapers there. His eye lighted upon an advert for a Kellogg Salesman, and he decided to apply. He was interviewed by W.K.Kellogg himself, who employed him forthwith and sent him out as a salesman in the States. His performance was impressive in the first year, and Mr Kellogg decided to send him back to England to set up the first Kellogg cereal-making factory outside America and expand the business from their small presence with one office in Bush House in London, two vans, and a secretary. He had finally made it!

The second of these two wonderful people, Lily Maude Hills, was born exactly three months after the conclusion of the First World War on 11th February 1919 in Southend-on-Sea. Giving birth to this first and only child would tragically claim her mother's life, Rose. Rose was dearly loved by her neighbours, who being deeply shocked by what had happened, took in the adorable new baby and looked after her until she could go to stay with her grandmother. Grandma, up to Lily reaching nine years old, provided a happy and stable home, but then she too died.

Meanwhile, her father, who was in the army, by this time had married again and had two young sons when Lily went to live with him and her stepmother. Unfortunately, he caught the Spanish Flu, a pandemic of the era, and died quite young. Lily's stepmother did not want her at all and became very cruel, hitting her regularly with an iron poker (used to stir up and adjust the fuel burning in the fireplace) and constantly shouting abuse at her; it must have been unbearable.

Amazingly, because the neighbours knew of the appalling treatment Lily was receiving and being upset by it, they complained to the authorities, a step practically unheard of at that time, and she was taken to the National Children's Home for Orphans in Oxted, Surrey. Much later, many people criticised the care in such homes, but Lily said it was really wonderful to be safe with other children and looked after by women who were kind to her. She often used to describe her first year or two in an institution as very strict and lacking in comforts, but then the founder died. After that, everything improved hugely. The girls enjoyed a higher standard of living, being well dressed, kitted out with uniforms, and allowed to attend the local school. When they reached fifteen years old, they usually went into service, i.e., they became maids or servants in the houses of the upper and middle classes. Lily had put on weight and seemed unlikely to be chosen by an employer, and once she became seventeen, it was causing real concern. She had to work extra hard to justify how much she was costing to be kept at the children's home.

It was around this time that our destinies met. My mother having had a heart problem since birth, was still fragile a year and a half after I came into the world while my sister was eight years old and at school. So my father went down to the Labour Exchange (now Job Centre), desperately hoping to find someone to help in the house. He remembered being advised that there was one young person looking for work before being taken to the room where Lily and her Guardian were waiting. He never forgot the radiant smile which spontaneously spread over Lily's face the instant he saw her. Without hesitation, he said he would like her to come and live and work with our family. To his surprise, the Guardian who had brought Lily for the umpteenth time and was used to her being humiliatingly rejected said, "Are you <u>really</u> sure you want her?" Cattle and slave markets came to his mind.

Lily came to our house for the first time on April 1st, 1937. She always insisted her arrival was after midday so as not to be an April Fool! She said it was seeing me trying to learn to climb the stairs that made her think how lovely it would be to live where there was a baby and with a family too! Of course, this is what she did.

Lily was happy to be part of our family even though she was working as a maid. In the morning, she wore a check pattern cotton dress mainly covered by a huge white starched apron, a white starched belt, and on her head, she wore a white starched cap. Starching, besides stiffening a garment, made its texture look better and crisper. After lunch, she had a break for a couple of hours, then reappeared at 4 o'clock in a silk dress with a pretty lace apron and a small lace cap. In order that she always had a clean and prepared set of clothes ready, she had two or three outfits of each type. All this was traditional for girls and women in service, but later it was considered demeaning. Refer to the popular television series Downton Abbey before passing judgement!

Around the same time, Lily's role began to be even more essential as my father's work was becoming more involved such that he was regularly away from home, initially investigating possible sites for an enormous new factory and then overseeing the building of it. The chosen location was Stretford on the outskirts of Manchester, which unlike the original choice of Slough, was close to the Manchester Ship Canal as well as railways and roads.

Once the green light was given for the £500,000 breakfast food plant with the prospect of a war on the horizon, construction work went ahead with unbelievable speed, even by today's standards. On 24th June 1937, the Mayor of Stretford put the civic seal on the pouring of the first concrete, which would be heavily reinforced throughout with high tensile steel as a safeguard against future air raids, and his senior equivalent, the Lord Mayor of Manchester laid the foundation stone thus marking the start of the building project, which was completed was in an unbelievable eight months.

With a new workplace being established so far away from where we were living, our house in Putney was no longer viable as the commute for my father was horrendous. Remember, there was no M1 or other motorways in 1937. Lily told me the tale of how utterly miserable and frantic he had been searching for another home. Rather disconsolate, he was driving along the A6 between Levenshulme and Stockport when he noticed an ominous black cloud forming above and behind him; there was clearly going to be a big storm very shortly as if things were not depressing enough! Suddenly, on the left, he saw someone in the front garden of an interesting house putting up a "For Sale" sign. Thinking he might be dreaming, he decided to turn the car round and investigate. He went up to the front door and rang the bell. A woman came immediately, and my father asked, "Is the house up for sale?" The answer came, "Yes, it is. I have only just put up the sign and managed to come back before the rain." My father was invited to look round, liked what he saw, details were exchanged, an offer of £800 was made and accepted the next day. Thus a seemingly insurmountable situation was resolved in the twinkling of an eye. Not long after the great move to the North of England took place, and once we were settled in at the attractively named Melrose on Wellington Road North in Stockport, all thoughts were directed to getting the new Kellogg's plant up and running.

My father and his team of directors felt that what was and still is the largest cereal-producing factory outside of America should be opened by someone very special. So rather than using the age-old selection of a celebrity, dignitary, or other VIP, they hit on the brilliant concept of finding "Britain's Typical Housewife" for the role.

"No more appropriate person could be found," explained my father, "representative as she would be of the host of everyday consumers of Kellogg's foods." These memorable words and what was a masterstroke of public relations were lapped up and loved by the general populace as well as the media. Backed by a leading Sunday newspaper, a nationwide search began, and soon, over five thousand entries came flooding in from all corners of the United Kingdom.

This huge number was whittled down until there were just nine finalists, all of whom were subjected to surprise home visits and interviews. For her amazing skills in feeding, clothing, and caring for a husband and six children on a meagre weekly wage of under £3.00 was regarded as all the more impressive because of her resourcefulness in baking her own bread, mending shoes, making things to wear, decorating and still being a happy woman, the winner was announced as a forty-year-old miner's wife from Mansfield, Mrs Florence May Millward.

Before hundreds of company and industry, and civic VIP guests from both sides of the Atlantic, the unveiling of a plaque that was fixed to one of the gate pillars at the entrance, the factory was officially declared open on 24ᵗʰ May 1938 by Mrs Millward immediately after she was presented with a bouquet of pink carnations by my sister. Sadly, unlike my sister Pat, because I was only two and a half years of age, I was greatly upset at not being allowed to go to the opening of the factory and instead being left behind at home with grandma and Lily, who were to keep an eye on me and provide entertainment. Rather naughtily, I decided to create a diversion by pushing an ornamental bead up my nostril. It swelled dramatically, but of course, it was not very comfortable and caused a panic for my carers – and me. All efforts to retrieve it failed, and in the end, our G.P. came himself to pull it out.

After the opening of the factory in north Manchester, which gave a euphoric local population the opportunity for new and extra well-paid work, we were all going to America to see the man who had made everything happen for us, namely Mr W. K. Kellogg. Even now, I can still remember the huge excitement of new clothes and shoes, packing suitcases, and preparations being made for the voyage across the Atlantic. Sadly, all plans for this wonderful trip were cancelled due to the Munich Crisis. This was brought about when Nazi Germany demanded the annexation of the Sudetenland, the Czech territory bordering Germany. The latter was one of many unpleasant hostile occurrences over a twelve-month period that formed the run-up to the Declaration of War by Great Britain in September 1939.

In the meantime, anxiety levels were very high, and the stress was transmitted to the children, unintentionally, of course. Discussions took place about my sister and me going to live in the United States of America in response to numerous warm, generous offers of hospitality from my father's friends and Kellogg contacts. As my sister and I cringed at the prospect because crossing the Atlantic was so hazardous, my parents decided we would and indeed should stay together. What effect it would have had on Lily is anyone's guess, as whenever my parents or all of us went away, she cried her eyes out for days beforehand.

In February 1940, Lily had her 21st birthday, and I remember we all went to the jewellers in Stockport to choose a gold watch for her to mark this milestone. She was absolutely thrilled, and it is probably true to say that this cemented her position in our household and family.

Despite being settled and extremely contented with her situation, Lily had a further threat to her existence when she received a letter calling her up to be a Land Girl. Not only was she disturbed by it, but also, my father thought that she had suffered enough insecurity in her early years and was just beginning to recover from the battering she had had both figuratively and literally. Despite being only twenty-two years old, she was a vital member of our household because he was away a lot of the time on business, and my mother's health was precarious. Last but not least, my sister and I were school age and could not shoulder such responsibility.

Looking back, it was absolutely right, I think, when my mother was in bed recovering from both heart attacks, and we had childhood illnesses like measles and chicken pox one after the other. Lily did all the cooking and looked after my mother and us. Fortunately, to Lily's great relief, the authorities agreed with my father, and she stayed at home with us, doing a fantastic job. She was a willing learner, one hundred percent reliable and honest. While she was in the National Children's Home, they had a visitation from the Rechabite Friendly Society to draw attention to the perils of alcohol and temptations in the world outside. This organisation was amazingly established several centuries before the birth of Christ by a Kenite called Rechab, from whom a tribe known as the Rechabites derived their name. He also had a son called Jehonadab. Jehonadab and his people all along became worshippers of God. He forbade his descendants to drink wine or to live in cities such that they were always commanded to lead a nomadic life and, where family was concerned, to adhere to fidelity. As a reward for their fidelity, God proclaimed that there would always be a descendant of Jehonadab in his service.

From Biblical times throughout the ages, many individuals, groups, or religions in different countries have professed to fulfil the latter role. The most prominent of these was probably the Independent Order of Rechabites or Rechabite Friendly Society, a Christian organisation founded in England in 1835 as part of the wider temperance movement to promote abstinence from alcoholic drinks.

Although it continues to promote abstinence because of its connections in upper society, it has become more involved in financial matters, and to reflect this, since 2004, it has traded under the name Healthy Investment (a with profits, mutual insurance organisation specialising in providing ethical, tax-exempt and other savings plans and investment products, not restricted to teetotallers with the emphasis on having no dealings with companies in the alcohol, arms, tobacco, gambling and pornography industries). The girls were invited to sign up for lifelong abstinence. Lily did this and never broke the oath she had taken for the whole of her life. It was something I have always been mindful of in terms of my own negligible alcohol intake.

As far as I am concerned, Lily was an amazing influence on my life. It was very lonely, apart from the time at school, and she spent hours helping me with my homework, playing all kinds of games with me that she had learnt in the National Children's Home, card games in particular and Beetle or Battleships. A firm favourite was general knowledge quizzes like Bird, Tree, Flower, Fish etc., the list of possible categories was very long, and then one of us chose a letter, and we got started! In the home, she had been a Brownie and then a Girl Guide and intrigued me with tracking, the Morse code, deaf and dumb language, and of course, we read books together like Beatrix Potter, a local resident who was still alive and writing her enchanting tales whilst being a farmer in Near Sawrey and reclusive, Little Grey Rabbit, Mabel Lucy Attwell, and later Enid Blyton to name but a few.

Thursday afternoons were supposed to be Lily's time off each week, but she rarely wanted to go anywhere, and it was a cause for concern to my parents. They insisted and encouraged Lily to go out. Fortunately, she was befriended by someone called Enid, who came from Ulverston but must have been working in one of the houses in Bowness. It emerged that Enid's mother was in a mental asylum, as they were called then, in Ulverston, and one Thursday, Lily went with Enid to see her mother. It was a disturbing experience, and Lily ventured the comment that the inmate did not seem to be mentally unstable. How right she was because sometime later, there was a national enquiry into patients in such institutions and a comprehensive review of their cases. It was revealed that Enid's father wanting to be rid of his wife, had her Certified Insane and committed her to the asylum. Found to be of sound mind, she was released forthwith and free to try and rebuild her lost life. Where to start?

Lily, when we returned to south Manchester in 1946, re-joined the Girl Guides rising to the rank of Lieutenant. Then she joined the St John Ambulance and was extremely successful in that organisation. Subsequently, she chose to emigrate to Australia with my parents in 1969 and remained with the family until my father died in November 1984 in the Isle of Man. She bought a house there and stayed for a couple of years before returning to Australia in 1987. She died there in 2004, having been a very lovable and remarkable person who was truly an inspiration to us all.

STOCKPORT TO THE LAKE DISTRICT

N ight after night, we put up with the eerie sound of wailing sirens signalling an urgent need to take cover, the fascinating yet terrifying fires lighting up the heavens as well as seeing the silhouettes against the skyline of the alarming large barrage balloons moored over Manchester and its environs which included our house in Stockport. We were constantly reminded of our risky position as I was carried down wrapped in an eider down by my father followed by my mother, my sister, and the ever comforting Lily to the air raid shelter. However, as we waited petrified for the menacing drone of enemy aircraft and their subsequent incessant bombing, he feared that we could be trapped because the entrance and exit of our refuge were one and the same, so he had the cellar of the house reinforced. He had beds to sleep in, which was much better, but still worried about a direct hit. Then, by July 1940, as if swiftly borne away by magic, we were suddenly living in the rather quaintly named Old England Hotel situated in the small town of Bowness-on-Windermere while my parents frantically looked for somewhere to rent. This heavenly haven of peace and tranquillity was a traditional English establishment in a prime position on the shores of Lake Windermere.

As fugitives from the onslaught of war, we received a warm welcome from the hotel staff, and they spoilt my sister and me with plenty of attention. Dinner, from what I recall, was served at 7.00pm, and on the first floor landing, there was a huge brass gong which I was invited to bang the agreed number of times. It was very exciting and reminded me of J Arthur Rank's introduction to his films. Many years later, when I was married with a son of fourteen years who knew the story, we were amazed to find the gong was still there, and he was allowed to bang it too. It was by then a Trust House Forte Hotel and visited by Sir Charles Forte while we were staying.

Something else that I remember was one day when we were having lunch in the restaurant that is to say, my mother, sister, and me, our table was on the next line of tables to the windows overlooking the lake and Bowness Bay. One window table was occupied by two ladies who we later discovered were mother and daughter. They were in earnest conversation. As I was looking at them, I saw a bee alight on the spoon of the younger woman just as she was about to put it in her mouth. With no time to ask my mother, I shouted, "Stop! There's a bee on your spoon," which she saw immediately and was totally shocked. It would have been painful and damaging to anyone, but this lady turned out to be horrendously allergic to bee stings! They were very grateful and made a big fuss of me, as did the dining room staff.

Later at dinner, there was a box on our table carefully wrapped and tied with ribbons – it was for me and contained an adorable, tabby toy kitten with blue eyes and a bow to match. I have been crazy about cats and kittens all my life, and this kitten went everywhere with me for a very long time. I still have it.

The ladies lived locally, and we became friends. The father and husband I called uncle George; for children, it was common practice with people of an older generation at that time.

Bee stings and toy kittens aside, despite the overwhelming anxiety as well as insecurity at the time because of the war, my mother, taking as our role models the two royal princesses Margaret and her older sister Elizabeth our present queen, was, for some reason obsessed with me and my sister aged 4 and 11 having white angora boleros. I think it was to try and focus on something pleasant for her children and keeping up high standards amid the turmoil of uncertainty. To see if there was any precedent for the sudden obsession that my mother had with white angora boleros, on researching, there came to light an article written by a stylist in 2011 saying brides-to-be were desperate to find the white angora bolero following the Duchess of Cambridge's unforgettable appearance at the time of her wedding in a McQueen gown with a jewel-encrusted waistband completed by a white angora bolero! The stylist was inundated with requests and at her wit's end when someone gave her a lead to Monsoon, which supplied exactly what she wanted in the nick of time. So the obsession with the white angora bolero is as popular now as it was then.

Usually, we wore velvet dresses with lace collars at dinner time in the hotel restaurant. My mother took us to all the outfitters in Bowness and Windermere to no avail while my poor father waited patiently in the car. Then someone gave her the name and address of a lady in Bowness who might help. Her name was Beatrice Hadwin. She lived in an apartment off Crag Brow in Bowness. The entrance was dark and daunting, as was the centrally placed lift, which had iron gates and lots of cables. We rang the bell, Miss Hadwin came to the door, and her personality lit up the premises, much to our relief. She was a beautiful woman with blonde hair, face carefully made up, and I was riveted by the bright blue mark on the bridge of her nose. It soon emerged she had acquired this and her artificial leg when she had gone to wave goodbye to her husband Daniel, who was leaving for the Front in the First World War, where he would later become a casualty or fatality, as we say nowadays at Ypres on 18 May 1917 aged just twenty-four years.

Overcome with emotion as she walked across the barrow crossing between the platforms to the station exit, a train coming in the opposite direction knocked her down, and she sustained critical injuries. Undeterred by her horrendous disability, she earned a living by making cosmetic creams and other beauty products. And yes, white angora boleros, which would be ready in two or three days.

Something else that I remember clearly which we did while we were living in the Old England Hotel in 1940 was to go on a glorious day tour of the fourteen lakes in the Lake District. From the garage near the Hotel, my father and mother hired a car that had cream leather upholstery, was immaculate, so comfortable, with plenty of leg room as well as having courtesy seats for me and my sister. The chauffeur was our guide for the day. Being so close by, it was assumed we would have plenty of time to explore the wonderful Lake Windermere, so we headed straight off to Esthwaite Water. When we saw it, Esthwaite was a beautiful, private location known primarily for its fishing. Set in a glacial valley, it lay between Hawkshead village to the north and Grizedale forest in the south. Over on the Eastern side, halfway along, it was also umbilically linked with Lake Windermere by a stream called Cunsey Beck which by coincidence emerged next to

Segrave's boathouse opposite the house where we would shortly be going to live.

Soon we were off to what I thought was the delightfully sounding Coniston Water, famed for many reasons. Its very picturesque setting we were given to understand was what attracted W.G. Collingwood to write a novel "Thorstein of the Mere" about Northmen who settled on Peel Island, one of two in the lake, the other being Fir Island. He was an antiquarian and secretary to the Victorian artist and philosopher John Ruskin, who lived at Brantwood House on the eastern side of the lake. When he died in 1900, age 80, he was buried in the parish churchyard, as was the late 19th and early 20th-century artist Henry Robinson Hall who moved to the area during the First World War. Here too resided another creative genius and favourite author of my sister's, namely Arthur Ransome, who wrote Swallows and Amazons along with its sequels Swallowdale, Winter Holiday, Pigeon Post and Picts and Martyrs, etc., based on school holiday adventures in the 1930s using loosely disguised but recognisable, local countryside and landmarks. The final occupant of the area of note was Malcolm Campbell, who used the lake to set a world water speed record of 141.74 miles per hour in his craft Bluebird K4 on 19th August 1939. His later trials had fatal consequences.

Nestled in the grounds of a nearby large hall, which took its name from the lake sequestered from the public at just less than a mile long and of irregular shape, was the diminutive Rydal Water. We had it reliably explained to us that its claim to fame was while the others are still wind-tossed water open to the elements, it was the first to provide bearable ice in the winter which is due to the surface being so sheltered by hills that it freezes. Some years later, my sister went skating there with our school teenagers and

Roedean girls too. Almost a mile beyond, we reached Grasmere, and we were informed it was a beauty among the lakes which was mainly known because one of the two boat landings at the edge of this small expanse of water called Wordsworth's. It was used by the poet when he lived at nearby Dove Cottage, the other being at Pavement End on Langdale Road.

In sharp contrast was Wastwater, which was unforgettably sinister with its sheer dark screes on one side, which went straight down into the water to, legend had it, a bottomless depth. We were told that witches were thrown down these screes into the water to disappear forever into the black depths, the murky frightening nature of which soon paled into insignificance as we left them behind, and lunch was starting to become foremost in our minds. We stopped at a hotel in Seascale, which was right on the beach, later to be the location of the nuclear power station, Windscale.

Seascale and Whitehaven, so our guide and chauffeur explained to us, were part of a very ambitious scheme to provide the two towns with a decent water supply by raising the level of the lake at Ennerdale, which was not only ideal since it had the purest water but also because it was cut off by high passes and tortuous roads from the area around it.

A few miles further on, secluded in a wooded valley, we came across Loweswater, which was a small peaceful lake of one mile in length, half a mile in width, and sixty-foot depth with only occasional visitors, according to our driver, and besides heading via Park Beck into the centre of the Lakeland, it drained into the much larger Crummock Water. A thousand yards wide and lying in a deep trough bordered by steep hills, it was affectionately known as the crooked one, taking its name from the curving nature of the lake as it led along to a southwestern inlet of The Dubs River, which joins the latter to Buttermere.

Buttermere, a small private lake at the bottom of the Honister Pass, bore the same name as the nearby village, so our guide was happy to tell us, and the Buttermere, Victoria and Fish Hotels had exclusive boating and fishing rights for their residents. Additionally, he regaled us with the story of Reverend Robert Walker. Reverend Robert Walker, besides brewing beer and founding the second of the three hostelries mentioned, on top of being a schoolmaster in the vicinity, took over a curacy at Seathwaite in Dunnerdale and then returned to marry Ann, his sweetheart. Sweetheart, so we learned, also applied to Mary Robinson, nicknamed the Maid of Buttermere, who was a shepherdess and the daughter of the landlord of the Fish Inn. She apparently married bigamously in 1802 a "Colonel Hope," the brother of an earl (so he falsely claimed). He was, amid much publicity surrounding the wedding, which included an account by Samuel Taylor Coleridge, subsequently exposed as John Hatfield, an impostor, bigamist, and forger. He was arrested, escaped, captured in South Wales then tried at Carlisle before being hanged in 1803. Mary's story captured the public imagination, and money was raised on her behalf. She married a local farmer Richard Harrison in 1807 and had four children before dying in 1837.

Approximately ten minutes away to the north by road was Bassenthwaite, a shallow lake which seemed to be a favourite of our guide with its attractive railway station known for its well-tended gardens that contained superb flower beds and ornamental bushes. With some camping coaches stabled in a siding there, often a feature at scenic locations, it was truly people friendly.

People friendly was certainly a really appropriate description for Derwentwater, too, as this particular lake, which included several islands within it, lay close to Keswick, and we were interested to hear it had become important to locals as well as nationals alike to the point that it was fiercely protected from overuse or development. Responsibility for activity relating to their precious asset became the domain of the residents of Keswick.

I recall Thirlmere in particular, which had very green surroundings. It seemed to be fenced off with high security, and the chauffeur told us that the lake provided the water supply for Manchester and so it was completely closed to the public.

Our last port of call was Ullswater, a lake surrounded by the villages of Glenridding to the south and Pooley Bridge at the northern end, and it was also, so we were informed, bordered by the communities of Howtown, Sandwick, and Watermillock. Most notably, it became popular with the British aristocracy as a fashionable holiday destination for themselves or when entertaining those from abroad, thanks to its good sailing conditions and proximity to fell shooting estates as well as regular steamer trips.

There were a few other lakes that we did not visit, such as Elterwater, Brotherswater, and Hayeswater, but that did not matter as we had enjoyed a really fascinating day with someone who seemed to have swallowed a guide book. Realizing that there would be restrictions on fuel for domestic car travel, my father had the idea of making the tour while it was still possible in order to get a feel for the area in which we were going to live but may not be able to see or visit for a long time. He was absolutely right because I was only four, my sister eleven, my mother could not drive, and we only had the use of a car if my father came home. There was no public transport except in the Tripper Season as it was locally named. These so-called Trippers were regarded with disparagement by the natives as they flocked to Bowness-on-Windermere for the day, probably from the factories in the summer months. Who could blame them, and to be fair, could they have afforded to stay anywhere when most accommodation had been requisitioned by the War Office?

DICK INTAKE

It was not just for us primarily but with the intention potentially of some office staff being able to continue to function if the factory was bombed that a month after our arrival in Bowness-on-Windermere in the idyllic county of Westmorland, we were able to transfer to a stunning rental property, Dick Intake, which sat at the end of a long drive in seven acres of amazing grounds. A large and imposing house but not pretentious, it was specially built of Lakeland Stone by a gentleman called Dick Eaves, who was the head of a large Catholic family with eight children based in Blackpool so they could spend school vacations there with staff. The atmosphere within the house was happy, I felt, probably because of the children spending their holidays there and borne out by the fact that they, now grown up, came back to visit whenever they felt like it. Helen, the youngest daughter, stayed with us sometimes. I think she was a little older than my sister. It must have felt strange to her to be in an old familiar place but with completely different people though we loved her visits.

On the first floor of Dick Intake, there were three large bedrooms, all with fireplaces and washbasins and a bell to summon someone from the kitchen. There was also a smaller room which was usually mine, but it did not have the same facilities that the others had. Additionally, the house boasted a huge airing cupboard (not surprising for such a large household) and the family bathroom with a separate toilet next to which were the stairs leading to the three large attic rooms above. A flight of service stairs existed, which were lino covered and led straight down to the kitchen. Thus, staff did not need to use the main staircase. There was a door over the entrance kept safe by a retaining catch at the top. On one occasion, I decided to use this direct route to the kitchen myself, so I reached up to release the catch, not knowing that someone had left it open. Of course, the door opened as I reached up, and I fell down quite a few stairs before managing to save the complete fall by catching the handrail. It gave me a terrible fright and, when she knew, my mother too. After that, it was kept locked!

On the ground floor, there was a dining room and two lounges, all with fireplaces. We spent most of our time in the brown lounge, as we called it; it was a cosy room always with a log fire, and we ate our meals when we came home from school at an occasional table where we also did our homework unless I was in the kitchen. The other lounge, which had the Adams ceiling and fireplace, was much more formal; our grand piano was in there, and we practised our scales and piano pieces in there, although it was normally pretty cold. Leading off this room was a door to a wing that must have been added some time later. There was a very large bedroom, a smaller room at the end of a longish corridor, and a bathroom and toilet presumably for guests. The bathroom water had a peculiarity in that it often came out like tea though I could not tell you why.

Between the two lounges were some rather grand ornate double doors leading out into a large conservatory. My mother, as a very keen grower, was suddenly in her element and set to work almost immediately with her magical green fingers. It was not long before the space was kept full of flowers and plants.

The area of the cultivated garden was huge with a basic pattern, a rockery, a summer house, a terrace, and in a separate area, even an aviary with canaries, budgerigars, etc. Once, I remember, I found a pigeon on the ground near the aviary, which seemed not to be able to fly. I saw it had an identity band on its leg and went to tell my mother. She knew straight away that it was a carrier pigeon that had become exhausted, and we would have to notify the relevant authorities as soon as possible because it was clearly on a war mission. Our instructions via the neighbour's phone were to try and revive it and let it fly off when ready, or someone would be sent to collect it. How smart of that pigeon to land near the aviary to draw attention to its plight.

The views were spectacular, with Coniston Old Man and Crinkle Crags in front of us across Lake Windermere, and Sir Henry Segrave's boathouse for Miss England was opposite. At the Ambleside end, we could see Helvellyn. Behind the house were Lakeland Fells, wild, remote, and treacherous.

One of the Furness Fells, Coniston Old Man to the west of the village of the same name and the lake Coniston Water was I discovered also known as The Old Man of Coniston or just The Old Man. Old Man, contrary to popular belief, had nothing to do with an elderly chap but was a corruption of the Celtic "Alt Maen" and additionally derived from the Norse for a pile of stones or crag. This stunning mountain in times gone by had been the subject of extensive copper and slate mining activity, the abandoned remains of which, along with the associated spoil tips, still graced the northeast slopes. Now all that was visible were the little white dots of sheep grazing. Legend had it that on a clear day from the two thousand six hundred and thirty-two-foot summit, though sadly we never had that pleasure, you could see the Isle of Man, The Lancashire Coast, Winter Hill in the Pennines, Blackpool Tower, Morecambe Bay and most of the southern part of the Lake District.

Forming a part of two major rings of mountains, surrounding the Great Langdale as well as Upper Eskdale valleys at a breathtaking height of two thousand eight hundred and eighteen feet is the fell Crinkle Crags.

The quite delightful name suggests a reflection of the feature's physical appearance, which is a summit ridge with a series of five twisted or wrinkled rises and depressions.

Miss England II was one of three vessels berthed in a boat house on the bank of Lake Windermere and used by Sir Henry Segrave, an American who was born at the end of the nineteenth century in Baltimore on 22 September 1896 and drawn to England to pursue a career and his interests. As well as designing an aircraft for luxury touring which he hoped would go into production, he was primarily an early British pioneer of speed records setting three on land and one on water. Besides having the distinction of holding both titles at the same time, he was the first to travel at over two hundred miles per hour in a land vehicle. Covetous of a further achievement on water, a few months after receiving his knighthood, on 13 June 1930, he propelled Miss England II to a new record of ninety-eight point seven six miles per hour on Lake Windermere. In a bid to go faster, he embarked on a third run which ended in tragedy as his boat capsized at full speed, whether as the result of it hitting a large floating branch or, as some thought, a fault with the integrity of its construction. While the mechanic only suffered a broken arm after being thrown clear of the craft, the chief engineer was killed by the full force of it turning over and landing on top of him. Having learned about the fate of "his men" and that he had set a new water speed record in the few moments he had regained consciousness, Segrave succumbed from acute lung haemorrhages. Shortly after his death, the Segrave Trophy was established to commemorate his life and recognize any British person who demonstrates the most outstanding accomplishments on land, sea, air, or water.

A staggering 450 million and 20,000 years ago, igneous rocks and the last ice age, respectively, were responsible for the creation of Helvellyn, which is the highest point of a north-south line mountainous range with the same title lying between the lakes of Thirlmere and Ullswater. It comprises two aretes or sharp-topped ridges known as Swirral and Striding Edge. Striding Edge sitting prominently above forms the back wall of the steep-sided hollow Red Tarn. Red Tarn is a small lake high up which evolved when the glacier that carved out the eastern side of Helvellyn melted. One of its roles was a habitat for the very rare and endangered Schelly fish, while another was as a dam that used boulders to raise the water level some eight or nine feet in order to supply power for Greenside Lead Mine at Glenridding during the nineteenth century. Approximately fifty years earlier, the amazing physical presence and scenery of Helvellyn helped it to be one of the earliest fells to prove attractive to walkers and explorers. Among the first of such visitors were the poets Samuel Coleridge and William Wordsworth, both of whom lived nearby at one period.

Most of this knowledge I picked up from Lily, who, probably as a result of her time in the children's home and being an enthusiastic member of the Girl Guides, had a real thirst for such facts and imparting them to us. Alternatively, we would learn them as part of general knowledge at school.

OAKBURN

Going to live in the Lake District as a young child because of World War II meant having to go to school there, and I was due to start in September 1940, about a week or so before my fifth birthday.

My first day was unusual and dominated by lunch served in the dining room, which doubled as a classroom outside of mealtimes. The room was full of pupils and staff, and it was busy and noisy. I felt shy. Then one of the two headmistresses of the school said she wanted me to sit next to her on her right at the top of the table. I was too small to reach the table, so books and cushions were fetched to make me high enough to eat from the table. Once raised up and teetering precariously on the makeshift pile of items, a plate of food was put in front of me. Imagine my surprise and horror when I saw that the plate contained a rabbit head surrounded by a sea of gravy. Gravy, to this day, is something that I have always avoided at all costs. Other than running away, which would be difficult perched as I was on a heap that could topple at any moment, I had no idea how to cope with such a situation.

My experience of rabbits was of the cuddly toy variety only, although my sister had had a large rabbit which was in a cage in our garden in Putney and ready to come with us on the morning of our move to Stockport. Tragically everyone decided individually that he must have a meal before the journey, and he came to an inglorious end, which caused screams of anguish and recrimination, but he could not be revived. Aged five, I really did not know how to deal with this awkward situation and to remain on speaking terms with the headmistress whose presence loomed large so close to me. Fortunately, time was on my side as the room would have to revert to a classroom in a very short time. The offensive rabbit head was removed, and a milk pudding put in its place, with which I had no problem. I did have a hang-up in the next few weeks with the school policy, which said you must eat everything on your plate because people were starving, and food was in short supply. One other food-related incident comes to mind, which illustrated the desperate measures people would go to and the strength of feeling they had in wartime with food shortages and rationing.

Rationing was not wasting anything that could possibly be consumed. E.Atkinsons and Sons of Bowness-on-Windermere, the prestigious grocers, must have contacted the school with an offer of a bag of rice found in their cellar, which they could not sell to the public because mice had nibbled the corner of the sack! The first we knew about this was when one lunchtime, the usually very palatable (at least as far as I was concerned) milk pudding tasted strongly of Dettol. We discovered later that the school cooks had, as a precaution, rinsed the rice in Dettol before cooking it! Mercifully, I think the rule about eating everything on your plate/bowl was waived that day. Through fear on the walk to school in the morning, I tried to convince my mother that I did not feel well and could I go home with her. She fell for it a couple of times only, and then I had to face the daily ordeal on my own.

However, there were treasures to counteract the fear. The chance to learn excited me very much, and the first of these was reading. Miss Knox, the other headmistress, taught me herself, and I can still remember the joy of discovering that I could read the printed word. She was kind and gentle and very clever. She inspired me with a thirst for knowledge and encouraged me to start learning French when I was seven which I loved with a passion.

Returning to the food issues, my daily dread of not being able to eat everything on my plate became a reality on another occasion at lunchtime quite unexpectedly. I thought puddings were always good because I liked Tapioca, Sago, and Barley, but this particular day it was sponge pudding with dates and custard. The dates were obviously cheap and fibrous, and the more you chewed, like stringy runner beans, the more those fibres got bigger to the point I could not swallow them. Everyone else was allowed to leave except me, and I was told I would have to stay there until I had eaten everything! The tables had been cleared and wiped, and the pupils for afternoon lessons had come in. At first, I was upset and cried, tears falling into the dish in front of me, but then I felt very angry and defiant, and in the back of my mind I thought my mother would be arriving at 4.00pm to walk home with me. I did not think she would regard this punishment as acceptable when the dates were partly inedible. When the bell went for the end of lessons, someone took my bowl away. Nothing was said. I felt that I had won a battle and shown that even little people have a sense of justice, but I was not happy about it. My sister confessed to me that boarders, far from the majority of children at the school and of all ages, regularly asked her, begged her to take food they could not eat, and dispose of it on the way home. They had tin boxes for the purpose!

On the other side of the coin, and in their defence, before Christmas, Miss Brett and Miss Knox organised parties for us at school, and these were always magical and memorable, and the food was amazing. For me, the excitement was huge; taking a party dress and party shoes to school in the morning, and then after lunch, we were allocated a boarder's bed in a dormitory where we could sleep among the treasured teddy bears and cuddly toys and pyjama cases of our classmates who lived a distance away. There was a lot of chatter, then changing into our fancy clothes before going downstairs and making a grand entrance into the party world below. The rooms were transformed with candle lighting, Christmas decorations, and a feast spread before us. We played party games, sang, and ate heartily before, in our case, being swept home all too soon by a chauffeur with a hire car from Bowness, one of our friendly guys who answered emergencies and brought us messages as, of course, we did not have a telephone.

In connection with Miss Brett and Miss Knox, and Oakburn School, there are two people who should be included. One was a young girl called Hannelore Kamke, who was, I think, about nine or ten years old when I started there in 1940. She seemed to me a very lonely soul and rather daunting, not surprisingly as she was labelled German and disdained accordingly. I only found out in 2003 that Hannelore was from Gdansk and not Jewish. Miss Brett and Miss Knox, with typical generosity, had long supported the charity, Save The Children, who were protecting Hannelore when she had first fled from Germany to Denmark, a product of the Walkemiihle School, which was outlawed by the Nazis when Denmark was occupied by them. The school managed to flee to Wales but there, the staff who were German were interned, and the organisation subsequently disbanded. Hannelore was then adopted by Miss Brett and Miss Knox. I further discovered that Hannelore's mother had been bravely critical of the Nazi regime and had been persecuted. She escaped once, but inevitably she was captured and perished. Their father had lost touch with them. I look back and think that poor Hannelore should have been treated as a hero and realised how much she suffered from misconceptions about who she was.

The second person Ruth (Oppenheimer) David was a pupil at Oakburn when I was there, but she was my sister's age, and they were lifelong friends until her death in November 2015; after that, Ruth and I remained friends until she too tragically died in April 2020, in Leicester, a victim of COVID-19. See her wonderful obituaries in The Times, The Telegraph, and The Guardian. Ruth escaped to England on the famous Kindertransport and eventually gravitated to an Austrian hostel for Jewish girl refugees in Windermere and came to our school a 5 1\2-mile cycle ride every day. When the hostel closed, though, it paid off finding Miss Brett and Miss Knox as they took her in along with Hannelore. Ruth won a full scholarship to Bedford College London, and on graduation, she became a teacher of modern languages. After her retirement, she dedicated her time to the important subject of Holocaust education, giving talks in Britain as well as making annual trips to speak at schools in Germany where she would relate her story.

LEARNING TO SWIM

Exactly how old I was, I cannot remember, but one summer term at Oakburn, my parents were notified that swimming lessons were an option. These would take place at a location below the school which was one of the largish lakeside properties with a big jetty and a boat house that had been kindly loaned by its owners. So about mid-morning on a warm sunny day, we set out, a party of youngsters and some older girls with swimming gear, towels, and shoes because the stones on the bed of the lake were rather slimy and slippery underfoot. Miss Brett, I think, had come down by car, but we had walked straight down from the landscaped terrace then through the rough ground where there was a magnificent golden oak, onto the main road into Bowness, which followed the shoreline before moving inland a little to accommodate the houses and gardens which were our destination. In a commanding position, Miss Brett was already up on the jetty, complete with a loud hailer so she could 'boom' if necessary. She had in her hands a canvas loop which we put around our bodies, leaving our arms free to do the swimming stroke (which we had practised on gym benches and horses) in the water and got the feel of it. Meanwhile, because the loop was on the end of a sturdy rope, Miss Brett pulled you along at a steady pace, feet still on the lakebed below. Amazingly, I was very excited by this new experience, and it was not long before I was confident enough to lift my feet and do the leg strokes – I was swimming! I was so enthusiastic about it that when my father came home for a weekend, I begged him to help me so that I did not have to wait a week between lessons. He was a very strong swimmer, and it had saved his life before I was born. He was staying with relatives in their house on the shores of Lake Michigan and was swimming while the others were having drinks and socialising in the garden. Suddenly, he felt himself being pulled down into a kind of whirlpool. He tried to shout for help only to find that the onlookers thought he was waving to them! He remembered being desperate, sucked down repeatedly, and then thrown up and thinking his last hour had come. Finally, he mustered all his strength and managed to reach untroubled waters, exhausted. He swam gratefully back to the family, who said, "Oh, there you are Harry. Did you see us waving to you?!"

Learning of my enthusiasm to swim, he was more than happy to nurture it, and so we all set out for Grange over Sands on a Saturday morning he was home. There by the seashore, was a sea water swimming pool, and I could not wait to improve my new skills. On hand was a young, very handsome man called Douglas, who was an on-duty lifeguard and instructor. He became my hero, encouraging me with my breaststroke and teaching me to dive at first as in standing on the side of the pool with toes curled over the edge and arms stretched out in diving position, then falling in to be caught by him, who gave me super confidence. We went several Saturdays, and then on one occasion, he was not there; he had been called up! Summer 1945 was very hot. I still went swimming with the school, but sometime in the summer term, I became very ill with gastroenteritis. Six or seven people in

Bowness-on-Windermere died, and there were two theories – one was low water levels in the Lake caused by drought and the fact that sewage did not clear in the usual way, and the second was contaminated sausages. Although I favoured the second theory myself, we never swam in the lake again.

THE FOUR SEASONS

In the spring and summer too, since it was before the days of insecticides, the grass verges of the road we cycled or walked along to school and back were adorned with amazing and colourful wildflowers. Miss Brett and Miss Knox insisted we should be able to identify and name as many of them as possible as part of our general knowledge. Pat and I knew where to find wild violets and primroses. Even in the field and wood area of Dick Intake's land, there were drifts of wild daffodils in March/April time, just like Wordsworth described. His poetic imagery captured the glorious reality of the scenery.

A most memorable feature of our years during wartime in the Lake District was the weather and how it affected our lives. There were some really hot spells, and of course, because it was Double Summer Time (two hours ahead of Greenwich Mean Time) to assist with the war effort and land harvesting, it did not really get dark until 11.00pm or midnight, and as a child, I found it very comforting that people were out working in the fields until quite a while after I had gone to bed. How I wished I could be out with them.

Spectacular purples, reds, oranges, and yellows worthy of rivalling the fall in the United States of America, which I was lucky enough to experience when I was sixteen, were so typical of autumn in the Lake District, which turned into a riot of colour as the leaves yielded to the lack of sunlight before eventually being stripped from the trees during October and November by the strengthening breeze. In Miss Brett and Miss Knox's scheme of things, we had to know all about seeds and seed dispersal (allochory or anemochory), which were just as hard to write as pronounce as well as what was happening at the time of year. Inside the pupils' entrance gate were horse chestnut trees that shed loads of foliage so that we trudged knee-deep along the path to the school door. Picking them up straight from the ground or needing to remove their spiky green jackets first, there were rich harvests of shiny brown conkers of all shapes and sizes with which we had various games and competitions. The smell of the undergrowth and fallen leaves at this time of year was wonderful. It was largely caused by dew and rain. Rain, when speaking about the weather in the Lake District, was a touchy subject as it fell indiscriminately all year round and often for days at a time. We were quite often embarrassed when people came to stay and never saw any mountains at all because they were shrouded in thick mist.

The winters were fairly consistently cold, with lots of glorious snow. One year in 1894-5 in Queen Victoria's reign, Lake Windermere actually froze over with ice hard enough for people to skate on, have picnics, light fires, and be out on the frozen lake in large numbers. It was still talked of in the 1940s when we lived there, and some people could actually remember the novelty and excitement of it all. One winter, I remember my mother, sister, and I were told about a small tarn on the road going to Crook where you could skate. The first time we went, it was moonlight, and my father was with us for some of the time before being taken off by car to go to Manchester to the factory. He left strict instructions for us about safety, like keeping away from the edges if there were trees or bushes as the ice would be thinner and listening for any cracks or groans in the ice – it was quite dangerous but very beautiful and romantic.

My sister had been given some elegant leather skating boots, which I coveted because all I had was a pair of boys' sturdy boots with the blade fixed to the soles, hardly glamorous but durable, and they served the purpose. The next morning it was Sunday, and it was bright and sunny. My mother asked us if we would like to return before it thawed. We were armed with brushes to sweep off any snow, our skates, of course, and some food. It was a long walk past school as far as Ferry Knab, where the road was, which led to Crook, but we were very happy and excited to be able to practise our newfound skills at moving about gracefully on the ice without falling over. No one else was there, and we stayed several hours, encouraged by my mother, although she was not tempted to try.

Heavy falls of snow in the winter months meant we could toboggan. Guys at the factory had designed and made for us a sledge with steel runners and a ply-board top. It was very sturdy and got up at a good speed. The field in front of Dick Intake sloped down to the road and, after that, to the lake. The only hazard was molehills which sometimes turned us over into the snow, frustrating on what seemed a fast, smooth run, but it made us laugh a lot, and it was such fun.

OUR HOMEMADE THEATRE/ STAGE

My father, ever resourceful and enterprising, being mindful of his absence from home, which was frequent though not, of course, as prolonged and stressful as it was for those away on active service, decided that we should have a family project to work on together and he elected to make a model theatre. It started in a modest way with Meccano, using numerous metal strips, plates, angle girders, wheels, axles, and gears that were connected with nuts and bolts, but then it became much more ambitious and technical so that we learnt all manner of information about scenery, lighting, safety, stage production, etc. until after a time we were able to give shows to visitors. Back at the factory, several people who lived on the site a lot of the time became interested in designing and making more sophisticated parts for the stage, which was very helpful in lots of ways to them and us. Funnily enough, my sister had aspirations to become a stage designer for a short while. My father was constantly thinking up improvements and innovations to put in place whenever he was able to get home. Even my mother helped by making the tiny grand curtains and wing drapes and by covering the one-and-a-half metre high proscenium with purple velvet and braid around the stage aperture. The whole structure was on a strong trolley so we could move it around easily and store it in the corner of the dining room when we were not using it. Looking back, it was the kind of project which could involve the family or people unable to leave home because of the lockdown from March 2020 onward. I was generally in charge of the lighting for the various scenes, and we had a rheostat for making variations in the effects, the simplest being morning light, daytime, and sunset, but I tried to achieve more subtlety, for example, creating the illusion of distance.

We had a transformer that reduced the mains voltage to a safe level, and we were able to have a revolving stage and understand how it could work. We had background music to the shows, which involved making suitable choices for what spectators were watching.

I kept a letter my sister wrote to my parents and me when we were staying in Blackpool for a week with my step-grandma, i,e., my father's stepmother. Her sending us a letter was occasioned by an unexpected visit late in the evening from Raymond Eaves, the youngest of the boys in the owners' family of eight children with some army friends.

FATHER BURROWS

Father Burrows was the priest at the Roman Catholic Church in Windermere. My mother, sister, and I were not Catholic, but my father had been converted during the time he was a very lonely, homesick immigrant in New York around 1931. When he and my mother married in February 1926, mum had been a Baptist and changed to being High Church so that they could be on the same level at the start of their life together. My father had been a choir boy along with his twin brother Sam, and both were altar boys, so they took seriously their religious beliefs and involvement and more so after their mother's death when they were teenagers. So my mother was shocked and upset to find out that my father had taken a further step without consulting her, and it was a step too far for her. More than likely, this was the result of the traumatic happenings in the United Kingdom during the Great Depression, as I have said before, but it is worth repeating because of the devastating effect of events. Yes, there have been ghastly devastating periods in fairly recent British history apart from COVID-19 in 2020, as we all know.

My father was already a married man, and my sister was born in 1928 when his ship struck the rocks. He had been a popular and successful cloth salesman with a house in Bradford, but suddenly there were no orders or sales, and worse still, his father-in-law Enoch Wood, who was a prosperous mill owner with a posh house in an affluent part of Bradford went bankrupt and lost everything which is what happened to most other people in the country. He felt and was advised that going alone to the United States of America was his only hope for himself and his family left back home, and so it was! Anyway, we were left a divided family as far as religion was concerned, but my mother did her absolute best to compromise. Father Burrows was a case in point. I do not remember when he met us for the first time, but he took us into his fold, Catholics or not. He used to call us his angels, mum, Pat, Lily, and me, and he would cycle out to see us from Windermere at least five miles on a bike that was rather too small for him because it made his knees stick out and his progress rather precarious. We found him immensely lovable, and he was very partial to my mother's Yorkshire baking with a cup of tea. He would arrive unexpectedly but was always welcome because he exuded joy and warmth, however bleak the situation might be.

I remember he was sometimes hard to understand because he spoke too quickly and had very protruding teeth. Rumour had it that people came from way outside Windermere on a Sunday morning to his full Mass because he rattled through the Latin at a record speed and let them out earlier than anywhere else to enjoy their Sunday, but I prefer to think it was his personality and goodwill which were the attraction. We were once invited to lunch at the Presbytery en famille. Father Burrows had a housekeeper called Mrs Maher, I think, who obviously looked after him very well because he was such a good man. We had a delicious lunch, and it was an extremely jokey occasion. The dessert was one of Mrs Maher's apple pies, and my enduring memory of Father

Burrows is that as it was being served accompanied by cheese, he told us, "Apple pie without cheese is like a kiss without a squeeze"!

COOKY

Cooky, as we called him, was a man in his late forties, an employee of Kellogg's who came to live at Dick Intake with us for five or six months but outside in the orchard, in a wooden hut surprisingly, which we had used as a sort of summer house! I think the reason was something to do with tuberculosis. Tuberculosis, or TB as it was more popularly known, was then and still is a bacterial infection spread through inhaling tiny droplets from the coughs and sneezes of an infected person over a prolonged period. Typical symptoms include a persistent cough that lasts more than three weeks and usually brings up phlegm, which may be bloody, weight loss, night sweats, high temperature, tiredness and fatigue, loss of appetite, and swellings in the neck. Once some or all of these have taken hold, it mainly affects the lungs, but it can affect any part of the body, including the abdomen, glands, bones, and nervous system.

Understandably so, my father was paranoid because it was a scourge and treatable only by ultraviolet light and living in the open air as in a sanatorium; this was prior to antibiotics. Anyway, my father offered Cooky a chance to live 'the open air life' in a pretty primitive style, and he gratefully accepted. COVID-19 restrictions have reminded me of this particular episode in the hut, but Cooky came to wash in the butler's pantry, a kind of scullery just inside our outer back door, and he used an outside toilet; he was not allowed to come into our house at all. Mum and Lily must have made all his meals which he collected from outside the back door. Cooky had a family which he naturally missed, so we were encouraged to go and see and talk to him but keep a safe distance. He was seemingly forever jolly, which I found incredible as I was always dubious and worried by his Spartan existence. Years later, in 1968, at a dinner for two thousand people in Manchester marking my father retiring after thirty-three years as Managing Director of the Kellogg Company of Great Britain, a man sought me out and said, "I do not think you will know or recognise me." Before he could continue, I replied "Yes I do. You are Cooky, who lived with us at Dick Intake during the war. How wonderful to see you again." He had come to tell me that his health had been fully restored and that living in the orchard had been one of the best times of his life. He had already been to thank my father for giving him that chance and was now thanking me for having helped him to keep up his spirits. It was wonderful to see him again and hear his news.

The trouble was that once someone had contracted tuberculosis, wherever they lived became a health hazard for their families – everything from their clothes, bedding, furnishing, and even the walls could be contaminated. During the 1960s, I remember a neighbour of ours spreading their washing on the garden hedge and not realizing the significance until one Saturday afternoon quite late. I saw the same neighbour walking up the road on her own and stopped to offer her a lift. To my amazement, she said she was going to Peppard Common, and I immediately said, "That is near Reading, isn't it? The only reason I know is because the sanitorium is there." To my even bigger surprise, she told me that was where she was going because her husband, a handsome and seemingly healthy-looking man, had the flu and had not recovered well and consequently had been diagnosed with a return of tuberculosis which he had contracted in the army some years before. Despite the antibiotics, he did not recover. When his widow moved, the incoming owners of the house had every vestige of internal plaster and windows replaced.

A further poignant example of the severity of tuberculosis is of one of my classmates, Eileen, from January 1946–July 1950. She left at sixteen, two years older than me, as were all the rest of the class. She was very pretty, sweet-natured, as well as popular, and her sporting talents were always in demand for netball and hockey teams. Tuberculosis was already in her family, I remember. When I left school two years later, still only sixteen, I had to wait a year to take up my university place. My father arranged for me to go to Australia with my mother – a kind of gap year with a difference! My headmistress sent me a letter in October 1952 when we arrived and in it was the awful news that Eileen had gone into the sanatorium, poor girl. She never recovered.

MEDICAL CARE IN THE EARLY 1940s

It would be all too easy for people nowadays to take for granted the many services offered and the huge backup support afforded by the NHS even though there has been enormous endorsement and appreciation shown for the care during the first stage of the COVID-19 pandemic, but I lived my childhood without it until I was twelve years old and believe it was not at all good and not reassuring in any way. First of all, there was no protection from vaccination, generally. My mother told me that immunisation against Diptheria, a terrible dread, was offered for the first time when I was about eighteen months, the minimum age I think, and she said she agonised over whether she should risk it for me. However, she did, and I suffered no after effects other than a small scar on my arm. I met someone six years older who had contracted Diptheria and had been in isolation at a hospital in Leeds when he was three. The memory never left him. Each patient had a number, and every day the numbers of those who had died were published in the evening newspaper. Although I was so young, I can remember being immunised while sitting on my mother's lap. She was not surprisingly so worried. Also, because I had caught whooping cough when I was only ten months old and had nearly died, she was even more anxious about my ability to survive.

These days there is a reliable and well-tested vaccine, of course, and the only risk is that some people may not take advantage of it and endanger the whole process.

When I was seven years old, my sister caught measles; there was an outbreak at school. As soon as she became ill, I had to stay away from school and wait for the inevitable. I remember feeling very poorly with a high temperature and an irritating rash. My sister was recuperating, and so my mother moved me into Pat's bedroom, where there was a fireplace, and an open coal fire had been kept burning while she was ill. It was comforting to see the firelight in the night when getting to sleep was difficult, and the warmth helped too. When I was most ill, mum came and slept in the bed next to me. One night I woke up feeling a bit afraid. I prodded my mother gently and said, "I am asleep, are you?" and she replied, "Yes, I am asleep," which we both always remembered with amusement.

Remember, the fear was born of there being no antibiotics available then. There was a remedy that sounded like a remedy for animals called Fenning's Fever Cure which I can remember being given, and its not unpleasant taste. My father, if he was able to come back home on a Friday, would bound upstairs to see me and, placing his hand on my forehead would say, "Cool as a cucumber!" which I think was what he hoped for rather than what he could feel!

Measles made us miss a large chunk of the Spring Term, and then the following year, we had chickenpox – same routine and absence from school! I remember the nasty blisters on our heads and on our faces which dried into very itchy scabs. Mother told me emphatically that we must not scratch them or we would have scars forever. Being children, it was still very hard not to, but the farmer's son, Jack, who delivered our milk every day, said that

Sheep Dip was the answer, and he would bring some from the farm. He arrived with a bottleful the next day, and mum washed our hair in it. Somewhat drastic, but I really liked the smell of the coal tar, and it seemed to do the trick even if somewhat of a risk. Contrary to what I imagined, I did not end up growing a woolly coat!

Luckily for us, my mother's resolve was unshakable – she had lived with a congenital heart defect since birth, of course; her parents, Clara and Enoch, were told she would not live beyond sixteen years of age and must lead a quiet, restful life. I think the defect was a faulty valve because as a child sitting on mum's lap with my head on her chest, I could hear three clear, normal heartbeats and then a disquieting abnormal squelch.

Having married in February 1926, my mother gave birth to my sister in 1928. It was not easy, but she achieved it. Early in 1935, mum told me she was in Bentall's, the department store in Kingston, looking for the furniture department, and she was told it was through the baby department. There she saw the most gorgeous cot, a whicker cradle which rocked and covered with very pale pink hand embroidered organdie. It made an impression, she said, and she felt broody. Well, she might, as she was pregnant with me! Once discovered, a mixture of joy and apprehension took hold – she was thirty-four and high risk. King George's cardiologist was consulted, possibly because of where we lived – he came to our house to see mum and pronounced that the pregnancy must be terminated. My mother and father said, "Absolutely not!" My father went to Bentall's and bought the cot, although they could not have known I was a girl. I remember playing in the cot later on, and there are photographs of it.

One example of the precariousness of our wellbeing happened one Saturday morning, I remember. My mother was in the kitchen washing a fine cut glass in which to pour a pre-lunch sherry for our weekend guest, Dr Andrew McGill, who was our GP in Heaton Moor, Stockport, a bachelor we all liked very much. To mum's horror, the glass broke, making a deep cut at the base of her thumb. It bled profusely, but luckily, Andrew was on the scene immediately. The wound had to be stitched, but, of course, he did not have anything with him. He had to hold on to mum's thumb while my father drove hell for leather to Bowness (five miles) to the GP's surgery. They were not back for hours, and, of course, no communication was possible between us.

By comparison, last October, when I received a serious wound on the back of my wrist, in shock and bleeding uncontrollably, my son and I managed to stem the bleed – he telephoned 999, and an ambulance was here in five minutes. The crew hoped they could treat the wound here, but because it was too deep, they bore me off to the hospital with absolutely nothing, and because I had been on government shielding, I had not been allowed out of the house at all since March 12th, 2020, and our lockdown continued for almost six months until the end of August. It was completely traumatic, but I had the most wonderful care. The following day I had to return to the Plastics Unit for minor surgery. Everything healed in record time, and now only eight months later, you have to look hard to see the scars.

The only medical care available was the GP, Doctor Buckley, who had to be called out from Bowness (using next door's telephone), for example, to confirm our measles and chickenpox, so the school could be notified. She managed my mother's two heart attacks with visits and Digitalis (Fox Gloves) and Bella

Donna (Deadly nightshade) and bed rest, but all visits and treatment had to be paid for! I did not like doctors at all because I was afraid, I think, and it was not helped by a situation when I was ill with gastroenteritis in 1945. Doctor Buckley was called in the morning and was talking to my mother just outside my open bedroom door, telling her she would return in the late afternoon and if my symptoms had not improved by then, I would not last that long. Nice one, not! So I had been told at least seven people had died of it in the village, and she must have known that a nine-year-old would understand exactly what she was meaning. I was terrified but also defiant, which was probably a good thing and made me determined to survive. The associated anguish with a need for medical care would come to a welcome end when the National Health Service came into being on 5th July 1948 and transformed our lives profoundly.

MONEY AND VALUABLES

One of the big anxieties of wartime, as I observed even as a child, was how to keep any kind of financial security. My parents, born in 1900 and 1902, respectively lived through the First World War but as dependents, and not the breadwinners, had both then seen the terrifying downward slide into the Depression with all its devastating consequences. After a brief time of hope, another world war loomed and inevitably happened. I have mentioned elsewhere that my father was paranoid about a fireproof and reinforced Deed Box which I know contained, amongst other things, bank certificates and National Savings Certificates. Something else he thought was a good idea was to invest in high-class jewellery which nobody wanted to buy in the current situation they were in. Years later, when I was twenty and engaged to be married to a Classicist and Numismatist, I was introduced to a formidable collector of Greek and Roman coins who accorded me the exceptional privilege of viewing some of his recent purchases with my husband-to-be. His name was Harold Raby, and as a retired bank manager, he had thought up the idea of attending coin auctions organized by such highly prestigious institutions as Glendining's and Spinks during the war, taking the opportunity to buy at very basic prices because of low attendance figures.

His collection, ultimately worth a fortune, he left to Manchester University Museum. I had the privilege of making the card index from his huge purchase ledger prior to my husband compiling a volume of the Sylloge Nummorum Graecorum, and I saw entries like a gold stater from Sicily with a date of auction sometime in 1941 or 1942 and a purchase price 15 shillings (75 pence)! If my father was home at the weekend on Saturday morning, he used to take us in the car to Bowness-on-Windermere to visit a jeweller and fine art dealer called Kenneth Dawes, whose premises were near the top of Crag Brow on the right in what looked like a purpose-built, single-storey, dark green shop with bay display windows. Inside, it was very atmospheric, the walls hung with pictures presumably for sale, and then in the middle, there was a big counter with special lighting, which enhanced the precious stones under scrutiny. The owners were now the two Miss Dawes. Dolly was tall and willowy and wafted around. There was a pretty garden at the back of the shop, which she tended and often asked us to see it. It was full of poppies, and being high up on Crag Brow, it had a spectacular view over the lakes and mountains. The other sister obviously ran the business. She and my father got on very well, and over time he bought some amazing jewellery for my mother as an investment. I remember a large opal ring in a setting of small diamonds, a pearl ring which I think came from someone in Sawrey and mum particularly liked. Among a long list of items he bought there was a very distinctive diamond brooch with a large central diamond of good quality. My mother loved it, and as she was always smartly dressed when she went out, it was usually on the lapel of her suit/costume jacket. When she died in 1979 in Australia, my father realising that you could not safely wear jewellery in the United Kingdom anymore, rather than offering it to me, decided to sell it. Through his advisor, who sold it to a jeweller in Stratford upon Avon, he found out that Dennis Thatcher had bought it for his wife, Margaret. At first, we were not sure it was true, but then there it was – Mrs Thatcher, our former Prime Minister, also wore well-cut suits, and it was on her lapel. Wonderful! I had wanted to send her the original bill from Miss Dawes in the 1940s because it described and authenticated the quality of the diamonds, but I never did, unfortunately.

Another memory of the Dawes sisters was that for youngsters like me and my sister at that time, they kept a treasure tray of small items you could choose, and then if parents approved, it was added to the bill. Once I chose a small silver boot that Miss Dawes claimed was to commemorate the Duke of Wellington at Waterloo; I still have it. It polishes up beautifully, about five centimetres high and perfect in its detail.

There was one other jewellers and Silversmiths in Bowness-on-Windermere called Winders which was very well known and I think was still in business until fairly recently. A speciality was Windermere Jugs – I received three of different sizes as wedding presents. My father bought some large silver items from them as part of his investment programme, and it was always a wonderful experience from the atmosphere in the shop to the professional service of the assistant looking after us, not to mention the dazzling array of items on offer like silver tea services, i.e., teapots, hot water jugs, milk jugs, and sugar basins often disproportionately large because sugar lumps were very big at one time, not small cubes.

THE TELEPHONE BOX

Generally speaking, in wartime, there were no road signs or signposts and very few public telephone boxes. One particular loomed large in my life and that of my sister in that if my father was home with us any weekend, he had to keep in touch with the factory, and on Sunday morning, he would take us with him to this particular telephone box between Bowness and Windermere and put through a transfer charge call to the factory while we waited in the car. It always seemed to be drizzling or raining heavily, so there was nothing to see but wet fields and no mountains because they were shrouded by the mist. My son has always been intrigued by this because reports given and decisions made were critical. He googled it to find there is still a box there and space to park, but it looks very built up all around, not surprisingly after seventy-five to eighty years! Strange to think that it was such a vitally important line of communication for the years between 1940 and 1945. Talking of which, one Sunday shortly after VE day in 1945, my sister and I were waiting in the car, as usual, when I saw in the field next to the little parking area a large notice advertising the forthcoming visit of a circus, a traditional circus with a big top and in that very field in July. For some time, I had been besotted with circus life, and Lily and I had been reading books about the circus at bedtime. It seemed a magical atmosphere, and I was very excited to think that a real circus was coming to Windermere soon. When my father came off the telephone, he was enthusiastic too, and once we got home, mum agreed that we would go.

We did not know then that now the war in Europe was over a Kellogg representative from Norway was coming over to stay that same weekend. His name was Bill Frisch, probably in his forties, and he came from Oslo and was absolutely charming. He spoke English very well and told us that it was like a dream to be able to travel again freely and, most of all, not to be expecting a knock on the door at home any time of day or night from the dreaded Gestapo because he and many other men were in the Resistance Movement. It made me think as a nine-year-old that even though things were tough in this country, we had not been under that kind of threat as we so easily could at the time of Dunkirk (26th May to 4th June 1940), which saw the defence and evacuation of British and other Allied Forces to Britain using a flotilla of hundreds of small boats.

He thought where we lived was very beautiful, and we took him, like all our guests, for a walk on the fells. It was noticed that Bill picked some wild sage, rolled it, and smoked it! The next day was circus day, and he said he would like to come. Although summer, it was the worst kind of Lake District weather, pouring with rain, misty and chilly, and very wet underfoot. I was really too excited to notice, and if a bit steamy in the Big Top, it was an amazing performance with horses, trapeze artists, and some big cats. I was ecstatic. Then we noticed Bill's teeth were chattering, and he said he felt very cold. He finally had to admit that when he heard he was coming to England, his male friends had got together to find him some suitable clothes that were very inadequate. His shoes were the thin-soled dancing variety, and his shirt was only a front, my mother said it was a 'dickey.' I am not sure if he had socks even. We were all very shocked and immediately set about warming him up. My father produced some shirts for him and a warm jacket, and when he went to bed, he was thoroughly thawed out and thrilled that an expedition to our shoe shop in Windermere was planned for the next morning to buy some sturdy shoes.

We all contributed to the compulsory coupons. Bill was absolutely delighted and was able to enjoy the rest of his stay with us comfortably clad. A bonus of his visit for me was that he told us that during the years of Nazi occupation, to keep himself sane, he had concentrated on his stamp collection; he was a keen philatelist. At school, I had met a Belgian Jewish girl Nicole Noble, and we became good friends. She was a young fanatical stamp collector and had introduced me to that different world of swap books, duplicate books, identifying stamps and their quality, etc. Bill was surprised and pleased by my enthusiasm, and we exchanged stamps for many years to come.

My passion for the circus lasted two or three years, I think, because when we stayed with my father's stepmother Hannah in Blackpool, we regularly went to the Tower Circus, and there was a very handsome lion tamer with whom I fell madly in love. It was a family joke, but when we returned to our home in South Manchester, Belle Vue had a circus, and my father saw that his younger daughter's hero had an act there. He booked tickets, and we all went. It was very exciting. However, inevitably I suppose, sometime later, when my father checked where he was performing, he discovered that my lion tamer friend had been severely mauled by one of his lions. It was tragic but made me realise that perhaps those beautiful lions were not really happy to be taught and have to perform tricks for an audience. End of story! It had never entered my mind that cruelty could be behind the training of animals to be subservient.

OUR CATS

When we went to live at Dick Intake, we went there in the wake of Lady Olsen and her racehorse. There was a shed outside the back door of the house where the food was kept, and I remember there were huge holes in the wooden floor where rats had gnawed to gain access to the sacks of feed. We were appalled to find there were rival tenants. My father said cats would make short work of them, and he went out and returned with two cats, a brother and sister, Ginger who was half Persian, and his sister, Blackie, who was black and white shorthaired. I loved them both, of course, because I was born a cat fanatic, I think, but it was Ginger who captured all hearts. He was very handsome and a wonderful character. He came into the house every night at 9.00p.m. to sit by the fire after his rodent patrol duties, and it turned out he loved tea, so he always had a saucer of tea before curling up and falling asleep on the hearth rug. His sister died quite young, sadly.

We had other cats, but they lived outside like farm cats, and we never saw another rat which was fortunate because having been advised to put poison down when we had lots of them in 1940, we suffered a really bad experience that nearly occasioned our evacuating the house and returning to the Old England Hotel! Luckily, my mother in spite of her heart condition, was very determined and courageous. My godfather, the company accountant, had come to stay, and my mother explained to him what was thought to be the ghastly pervading pong. Together they came to the conclusion that a decomposing corpse was under the foundations of the house. As there was an access grid in the conservatory and on the outside wall of the house and it looked big enough for an adult human to crawl through, so off they went on hands and knees with torches. It was not far to crawl to find the source of the appalling odour and to be able to remove it. I do not think I could have been brave enough even to crawl into the underdrawing as mum said it was called.

One cat of which I was particularly fond in 1944-1945 was Kitty, a young tortoiseshell cat. I never liked the fact that the cats lived outside, and I spent some time thinking and planning how I might encourage her inside the house to sit by the fire, for example. After several unsuccessful attempts, I managed it, and she sat on my lap very briefly, but I soon realised she was more feral than domesticated, and when I gave her a chance, she made her escape. Sometime later, she disappeared. It was devastating, and we kept looking for her and calling her but to no avail. Fleming thought she may have been caught in a rabbit trap or snare. The number of rabbits was significant in those days, and they were a common source of food. I cringed at the snare possibility and thought of her, constantly hoping that she was unharmed. Several months went by, and then one Monday morning in late spring, we were all outside the back door ritually doing the washing when suddenly Kitty appeared looking very proud and happy, leading a little procession of four beautiful eight-week-old ginger kittens that she had reared in the wild. We and the other cats were all overjoyed. We easily found new homes for them, but they all, with

Kitty, their mum, lived in the house until they were ready to go, which had been my dream.

Thinking back, after the early days, we normally had between five and seven cats living outside and being fed twice a day. There was no commercial food available like Whiskas or Felix, so my mother and Lily made their food every day in addition to the hen food and ours, last but not least. Twice a week, they had lights, a sort of offal derived from the lungs of game and livestock which came from the butchers in Bowness and were cooked up on the Esse range. They did not smell very appealing to us, but the cats went absolutely nuts over them, and I understand they were very nutritious.

Ginger came with us when we left Dick Intake in early Jan 1946, and he slept on my lap the whole very traumatic journey. Amazingly, he adapted to the new house and town life, but what a lot to ask of him!

My desire to give cats, animals, and people warmth and comfort got me into a bit of trouble on one occasion. One very wet Sunday afternoon, the rain was pouring for hours, and one of the hens had a young brood of chicks in a nesting box in the hen house. It was quite chilly too. My father was home, and I am not sure whose idea it was, his or mine, that the mother hen might not be able to keep her chicks dry. Anyway, my father asked me to run across the field to Fleming's cottage and ask him if we should bring them into the house. I did not need to be asked twice and took off like a blue streak to knock on Fleming's back door. He seemed surprised when I asked about taking the chicks inside and said without hesitation, "No, no, they'll be alright, don't worry – and I'll be coming over later anyway to stoke the furnace." Between the cottage and our house and having got wet myself on this errand, I changed his advice and told my father that Fleming had said "Yes." The chicks were soon running round in a tray in front of the fireplace. I was kind of happy except for the nasty sinking feeling a complete and utter lie had passed my lips. Retiring to the safety of the upstairs to try and justify to myself what I had done and worry about Fleming's inevitable visit to check out the hens and fuel the central heating furnace. I remember hearing his knock on the back door, Lily answering, and Fleming asking where the chicks were.

Very frightened now and expecting a proverbial explosion, I went and hid in a cupboard in my sister's bedroom, awaiting discovery and punishment and, worse still, feeling I would never be trusted again. Strangely enough, I was trusted and given a chance to explain myself. Where I went wrong was saying that Fleming had said "Yes" when he said "No." The truth is always the best option I learnt.

DIGGING FOR VICTORY

Soon after taking up residence at Dick Intake and when my father was not there, the man who was initially employed to look after the grounds and lived in the cottage outrageously told my mother that you were still a foreigner unless you had been in Westmorland for a minimum of twenty-five years and furthermore, he would not take orders from a woman so she should not try. My mother was furious. We, that is to say, Lily, my sister, and I, finding him sinister and menacing, tried to avoid any contact if possible. One of our cats had just had kittens, and my mother was worried because they were outside and the weather was very wet. He came over from the cottage to stoke the furnace, and mum asked Lily to take a message to him to make sure the kittens were safe and dry before he left. Lily said he laughed, telling her he had done something with them so unspeakable that I cannot even write it after all these years. With all of us shocked and sickened, my mother charged out then and there to tell him he was sacked and must leave the cottage and our premises as soon as possible. Apparently, he thought of protest but knew the game was up. He was a thoroughly unpleasant individual whom we could not wait to be rid of. Soon after he left, my mother was told that there had been a daughter, and rumour had it she had been abused to the point where in her late teens, she had drowned herself in the lake.

We were intensely relieved to be rid of someone so evil and frightening, but of course, there was now noone to manage the grounds. Advertisements were placed, but such things took time, and meanwhile, there was a risk of fines if you did not cultivate the land and make it productive. During World War II, a phenomenal campaign known as "Dig for Victory" was established by the British Ministry of Agriculture, which produced copious propaganda leaflets encouraging men and women all over the country to turn as many places as possible, from domestic gardens to public parks where they could grow their own food ensuring that people had enough to eat and keeping morale high.

My mother was already walking to school with us every morning and meeting us at four o'clock. I can remember that we all went straight to the vegetable garden after getting home to do weeding and digging until it was dark. My mother, with her congenital heart condition, was resolutely determined to give her all. Exercise was probably not a bad thing for her, even if excessive, but I think it was the stress that went with it that occasioned her two heart attacks.

In addition to there being plenty of eggs and a copious yield from the huge vegetable garden, there was a massive fruit cage that contained gooseberry bushes, black currants, white and red currants, raspberry canes, and loganberry canes, and even a strawberry patch. My mother made jam and lots of fruit in Kilmer jars in season; she also made pickles, onions, onions and cucumber, piccalilli, and enough to be able to send some to my father's (Kellogg's) factory canteen.

Not only did we do as much as possible outside the house for the war effort, but also, we toiled away inside for our brave armed forces. "Make Do and Mend" was very much the order of the day also, and to this end, an indispensable pamphlet was distributed to households which was designed to provide tips on how to be both frugal yet stylish in time of harsh rationing. In addition, there were suggestions on reusing old clothing and how to make it appealing, like using 'decorative' patches to cover holes in worn garments. My mother, with the tailoring skills she had been taught, would do all of the latter as well as unpicking old jumpers to create re-worked fashionable clothing, while Lily, besides darning and altering items, having been supplied with instructions, would knit socks religiously.

How long it was before Fleming and his wonderful wife, Elizabeth came to live in the cottage, I cannot recall. He had just retired from his own farm in Rosthwaite near Ullswater and sold up. Having three daughters meant, unfortunately, there was no one to take the reins from him. This very intelligent gentleman was shy, having spent long hours alone behind the plough with horses only before any mechanisation. His wife was very practical and a lovely woman. She told us she had been educated at a tiny village school, but I still remember her beautiful, perfect copperplate handwriting and faultless spelling. By letters, she kept in touch with us long after Dick Intake days and until she died.

It was such a relief not only to have dependable people living in the cottage but also that we no longer needed to work the land since it was now being cultivated by Fleming, who, for me as a child, was just magic. He liked the fact that I was interested in the traditional farming skills that he had, and over time, he taught me drystone walling and a lot of other things about the countryside.

Although he was a quiet man, I found him very good company sometimes, a grandfatherly figure.

MEET OUR RELATIVES

Two of my real grandparents had already gone off the scene. Grandad on my father's side of the family had a sudden and fatal heart attack on New Year's Eve, 1940. As he and his second wife Hannah lived in Blackpool, a car arrived with a chauffeur who brought the tragic news, and he waited so my father could leave immediately to go and comfort her in addition to arranging the funeral. My father, not surprisingly, hated New Year's ever after. He was close to his father, his mother, and his twin brother. His mother had sadly died when they were young teenagers.

Clara Curtis, my grandmother on my mother's side of the family, was born in 1870 on 18th, November, and she was the eldest of twenty-three children, nineteen of whom survived – the last four were two sets of twins who did not live very long. My mother told me that when she was little, it was a wonderful house to visit because the boys, her uncles, made a gymnastics team that gave displays, and they taught her how to swing Indian Clubs, climb ropes and wall bars because they had turned the hall of the house into a gym. Every weekend the girls looked after the boys, and the next weekend, the boys looked after the girls. Great Grandad lived until he was fifty-seven only, a cabinet maker, but Great Grandma, aged 81, went to America, by sea, of course, to visit ten of her children who had emigrated, I think to Utah, but

I cannot be sure. Clara, my grandmother, married Enoch Wood, who had worked down the mines as a young lad and had been badly bullied because he was the son of the foreman; the boys used to push the trucks into the backs of his legs, so he always had painful heels and ankles. I do not know how he managed to rise above this to become a very successful and prosperous mill owner with several shops in Bradford selling cloth. He had a big house in Ash Grove, Bradford. My mother used to tell me that when Enoch married Clara, they did not have a honeymoon, so they went straight to live in a cottage somewhere near. The next morning Clara got up and as usual baked twenty-eight loaves of bread, not knowing how to adjust the ingredients for two instead of eighteen brothers and sisters. Enoch was shocked, but they borrowed a wheelbarrow and wheeled the bread to the family house, where it was not wasted. When I was a child, I never really got to know Enoch, and I do not know why but my father did not like him much either due to circumstances preventing him from inheriting the business or maybe because he thought he did not value Clara enough. By contrast, my father adored her. Pat, my sister, however, became very close to Grandad Enoch when he and Clara, as so many people tragically did, lost everything in the Great Depression of 1929. Grandma was allowed to keep a little jewellery, and that was all. My sister said that Enoch walked around like a lost soul gravitating to his allotment where he had some focus. I think my sister helped to preserve his sanity as she was always very sociable. This was long before I arrived on the scene in 1935, my sister having been born in 1928.

My father encouraged grandma to stay as much as possible since he loved her company and sense of humour. In 1936–1937 we had moved to a lovely house in Putney called Craigleith, which later became the home of the organisation for District Nurses. It was close to Putney Heath, where grandma used to take me for walks. Haile Selassie, the emperor of Ethiopia, used to walk there too with a servant/bodyguard who held an open umbrella over his master's head. One day Haile Selassie sat down on the same bench and started talking to grandma about comparative religion; she was a bit of a mystic. The next day the servant came round to our house with a bag of books sent by Haile Selassie, and afterward, they often had long conversations on the Putney Heath bench. Also walking on the Heath was a famous actor and heartthrob of the time called Ronald Colman, who thought I was cute, but I am sure it was grandma he liked talking to. I have a dim recollection that he came to my second birthday tea and had a piece of birthday cake (confirmed by my mother).

Poor Enoch, grandma's husband, when she came to stay which was quite often, was left to look after his cousin Lucy who not only had dementia but was also endlessly demanding. She had been a highly respected headmistress of New Brighton High School, trained and qualified as a teacher at Ripon College in 1888. When she left there, my mother told us that she applied for and was accepted as a governess for a child in a large house near Barnstaple. Her father took her and was satisfied with the place and the seemingly welcoming employer. Although we never knew if there actually was a child, he left her there to start her duties. It soon transpired that Lucy was a prisoner, locked in her room, terribly desperate and very frightened. The milkman, she noticed, passed under her window in his horse-drawn cart every day, and she managed to throw a 'help' note to him and a letter to post to her father. Luckily, the plan worked, and Lucy's father turned up unexpectedly to get her release. No follow-up explanations or recriminations happened in those days, but my mother maintained that Lucy was permanently damaged psychologically, if not physically, and she did not trust people, especially men, ever again. My mother said that her father thought investigation and scandal would compromise Lucy's chances of further employment. We tried to give my grandparents a break by having Lucy to stay with us for a bit, but unfortunately, she attacked me out in the garden, and my mother said she must go back home as soon as possible.

In January 1942, grandma came to stay for a break, and we had heavy falls of snow, lots of sledging, and trying to keep warm. As soon as the roads were passable, grandma went back to New Brighton. There were air raids, and shortly after, the blast from a bomb falling nearby brought down one of the ceilings in Lucy's house. For grandma, it must have been the last straw because she had a stroke and died shortly after. The news was kept from me so casually one breakfast time I asked when grandma was coming to stay again. My mother, as if stung by a scorpion, rose from her chair and flew out of the room, leaving my sister to break it to me gently that grandma would not be coming again. It was so very painful and so final.

HAIRY MOMENTS

As we did not have a telephone, living in a remote place with our father only coming home some weekends because he was heavily involved with keeping the production of food going that was essential for the armed forces and the civilian population, and our family 'temporarily' consisting of just my mother who had a congenital heart condition and suffered two major heart attacks the care of which had to be at home during the years we resided in the Lake District, Lily who was 21 and, last of all, us two children me aged 5 in 1940 and my older sister aged 12, besides feeling vulnerable, we were virtually isolated, to say the least, and life was not without its hairy moments.

Although we were sheltered from the war to a large degree while living in the Lake District, nevertheless, inevitably, there were constant reminders. One was that at night if we looked out of the bedroom windows facing the lake and to the southwest, we could see the fires resulting from the German raids on Ulverston and Barrow in Furness's strategic bombing of the shipyards there. Usually, at night if you woke up for any reason, the silence in the house and outside was intense. One night when we were all sound asleep and completely unsuspecting, suddenly the peace was shattered by the almightiest bang, followed by a thud on the floor upstairs, further bangs/explosions, and continuous shaking of the sash windows so violent that we thought they would fall out. Lily appeared in her pyjamas, looking pale and shaken; she had been blown out of bed! We found out later that a German pilot on a raid over the shipyards had missed his target, seen the lake in the moonlight, and decided to unload his bombs into the water opposite our house. Fortunately, we did not sustain any injuries or breakages, only shock!

Another incident, slightly less stressful, was hearing a lot of commotion in the form of noise and voices coming from the direction of the lake at about five o'clock in the morning. What was this disturbing and sudden frenetic activity disturbing the usual welcome silence? We looked out to see astonishingly a very large Sunderland Flying Boat floating on the lake outside. There was a factory of Short Brothers, the manufacturers between Bowness and Ambleside.

At first, it was thought that the Flying Boat, which had engine trouble, could be towed down the lake to Short's, but then it was realised that Belle Isle near Bowness lay diagonally across the water, making two channels too narrow for the huge wingspan of the Flying Boat. In the end, the wings had to be removed in order for the crippled aircraft to get back to base for repair.

One Friday night, when we were not expecting my father's return, it was about 9.30pm and very dark outside. Lily was sitting in the warm kitchen, and my mother, sister, and I were listening to the radio in our cosy sitting room with a lovely coal fire to sit by prior to going to bed.

Suddenly, Lily, hearing a vehicle coming down the gravel drive followed fairly soon after by the back door opening and a man's voice calling out "Hello, I'm back!" excitedly rushed to tell us, and we were all eagerly awaiting my father's appearance. There was no one. The back door was wide open. Some of the cats had come into the scullery rather puzzled with their fur standing up. On investigation, there was no sign of the vehicle. Disappointment consumed us but not as much as the dismay that no explanation was forthcoming. Had someone come to the wrong house and realised their mistake? Where were they now? Was it a ghost? Later we had to go to bed not a little worried and rather afraid.

A little worried and rather afraid were expressions that had to pale into relative insignificance, being replaced instead by confidence and boldness as there was very little entertainment that you did not have to make yourself, most of which was adventurous and daring. I became a wild child climbing trees, exploring the land around the house, talking to the red squirrels, and playing in the brook which ran off the fells through our woodland. I liked sawing wood, so my mother paid me a silver sixpence if I filled up a brass box we had by the fireplace with kindling wood for the fire, which was lit every morning. My sister and I sometimes spent time together, but seven years was quite a big age gap, and she was a dreamy teenager and an artist who did not like helping with domestic chores like I did, having a great love of washing floors, for example. Schoolmates were either boarders, or they all hailed from the opposite direction, Bowness or Windermere; the holidays were even more lonely. There was one occasion when I was about eight years old when it was lucky that I did spend hours wandering about in the fields and woods as well as "beating the bounds" of our seven acres of land. It was mid-afternoon, and something made me go down the field towards the road which went between us and our lake frontage before heading into Bowness. There was almost no traffic on it because of petrol rationing. I thought I heard groaning sounds. At first, I could not see anything, but then I noticed the big tree by the side of the road and leaning against it someone covered in blood so that I could not tell whether it was a man or a woman. A few feet away was a mangled bicycle. The spectre was frightening, but I knew the person was alive because of the groans. I shouted, "Hello, do you need help? I'll get someone as quickly as I can." A weak voice said, "Thank you." Then I ran as fast as I could up to the house to find my mother, who was, although untrained, a natural at first aid and caring for people. I worried because of the bleeding and not knowing how long before the accident had happened but doing anything was better than doing nothing.

My sister was despatched to our neighbour who had a telephone to call a doctor out from the village. An ambulance would have to come from Kendal a long way away but possibly still necessary if the injuries particularly to the hand, were serious enough. The injured person was in her thirties and mega relieved that I had alerted people to come urgently and not just run away with fright at the horrible sight. Several weeks later, having recovered, she came to find our house and to thank us, me in particular, for having raised the alarm. It was just lucky that I was out on one of my exploring adventures.

Another incident late in the war, about 1944, involved Fleming, the retired Lakeland farmer who came to live in our cottage and help maintain the land. He was out on the Fells behind our house one murky, dank winter's afternoon, a Saturday or a Sunday, when suddenly a young man rose up from the bracken where he had been hiding. Fleming was tall but thought he was being attacked, so he launched a counter-offensive whereupon the young man fell to his knees saying, 'Help me, Help me,' in broken English. It turned out he was a German Prisoner Of War (P.O.W.) who had escaped two or three days before and then discovered what a hostile countryside he was lost in. He was weak and desperate, soaking wet, hungry and thirsty, and very frightened. Fleming took him home to our cottage, where his wife made him some food and hot drinks and found some dry clothes for him. Then the police had to be called from Windermere. He had been reported missing. Statements were taken, and the young man expressed his gratitude and relief at having been recaptured. He would have died of exposure, no doubt about it. Fleming was hailed as a hero for capturing a German prisoner, but he modestly said in his droll way that it was more a case of him falling into his hands.

PRISONERS OF WAR

"All prisoners of war are equal, but some are more equal than others" Courtesy of George Orwell, and this you will see. The Lake District being a fairly remote location was clearly thought to be a suitable place for a Prisoner of War camp. Grizedale Forest Park lay over the other side of the lake, not readily accessible and quite isolated. We knew that German Prisoners of War (POWs) were kept there, and Italians also, but rarely did we see any of them except perhaps for my sister and me passing working parties repairing the roads under casually armed supervision. The Italians always called out friendly greetings to us – I am sure they missed their families. We smiled and waved to them but, of course, kept going on our bikes.

Food-wise, there were restrictions in the village shops, which we accepted as being general throughout the country. There sometimes were flurries of excitement, as in when a member of the armed forces came home on leave to Windermere and brought some lemons from a more exotic but hostile location. A lemon was put in the middle of the greengrocer's shop in Windermere for all to see because children like me could not remember what a lemon looked like! One day someone who had stayed with us on leave sent us a large pineapple through the post. It had travelled quite extensively, and for many days by the time it reached our house, it was over ripe. Our postal delivery man holding the shabby parcel at arm's length at the door, said, "I think someone has sent you a pineapple. Haven't smelt one of these for a very long time!" My mother's biggest moan was that there was very little variety at the fishmonger's here in Bowness in smoked haddock or dabs (young plaice). She used to get cross with us or pretend to when we would pat her face gently and say, "Is it dabs for tea?" Partly thinking we were being cheeky and partly out of frustration.

One Saturday morning, we were parked outside the fishmonger's as usual when my mother emerged in a flurry of excitement, saying to my father that she could not believe her eyes because the display slab was full of all kinds of fish, including turbot, halibut both pretty expensive but usually simply not available like lobster, etc. My mother, on asking the fishmonger from where this rich variety of choice had come, leaned over and whispered in her ear that Mrs Albertini, the widow of an Italian Colonel, had come to live at Grizedale and was entertaining the detained high-ranking German officers, Colonels, and Generals to dinner at her place Birkett Houses. What? The village was outraged, protesting vociferously that these were enemy prisoners. Why should they rate such luxury food? Perhaps Mrs Albertini was relaying information to be gleaned from small talk or dinner topics? Who knows? We used to hear some of the gossip from our Bowness-on-Windermere hire car chauffeurs whose firm had the contract for ferrying the Generals to and fro. However scandal it may have been, the standard of living suddenly went up hugely. After the war, apparently, Mrs Albertini married Colonel Veitch, and they lived at White Lodge in Windsor Great Park, which later became the Royal Ballet School.

Statistics show if it is really the case that only one German Prisoner of War ever attempted to escape from this country. I do not know if he succeeded. Most never wanted to and often did not return to their homeland after the war particularly if it was in the Russian Sector. There are famous examples who stayed, like Bert Trautmann, who divided his time between farming in Lancashire and playing football. In spite of quite long and chilling opposition from his supporters as well as his teams, St Helens Town was followed later by the famed Manchester City. Eventually, due to his excellent performance as a goalkeeper, the vociferous protests at the latter club deciding to sign a former Axis paratrooper were soon forgotten, and he gained a hard-earned acceptance.

WARTIME FUGITIVES ON ACTIVE SERVICE, MONTE CASSINO, AND D-DAY

With his very strong connections with America forged in the 1930s when my father himself was an immigrant seeking his fortune because everything here was in ruins and the future bleak when the USA came into the war, he gave our Lake District address to many of his former Kellogg Company Colleagues who had sons serving over here who could not go home on leave. Two were most notable for their personality as well as the historical significance of their visits. One was Rusty Gopel, whose parents left a message with our neighbours to say he may turn up to spend his leave with us while on active service in Italy. One night without warning, Rusty turned up at 10.00pm in one of the hire cars from Bowness. When we opened the front door, there stood in front of us a guy in a battered uniform, completely dishevelled and dust covered, holding out in front of him an equally dusty bottle of liqueur. "Good evening, I am Rusty Gopel, and I've brought you a bottle of Benedictine from Monte Cassino." With his comrades, he had been holed up for weeks in a cellar in the town below the monastery, then he had to leave to come to England and found the way to us. He had a lovely jolly, sunny disposition but was utterly and completely exhausted and traumatised by the experience of war at Monte Cassino from January to May 1944. He slept for hours but told us later he could not convince himself that the silence and peace of our house and where we lived were real and that he was genuinely safe from the ghastly risks and possibilities of being in the cellar in the thick of the fighting at Monte Cassino.

He explained clearly that the Battle of Monte Cassino was a succession of four carefully planned and hard-fought assaults carried out by a very large contingent of allied troops of different nationalities between 17 January 1944 to 18 May 1944 over what would prove for them a frustrating as well as gruelling four months.

Monte Cassino in central Italy (then a key ally of Germany), he told us, was a mountain on which stood an abbey above the town of Cassino through which ran one of the primary routes to Rome. Sadly, alternative routes were impassable because of flooding and harsh terrain (made worse by winter weather). To block this main and only potential thoroughfare, he said the Germans had established numerous seemingly impenetrable defences across it, collectively known as the Winter Line. Consisting of three parts, we had the Bernhardt line to the south-east, the Hitler line to the north-west, and then most important of all, the Gustav line into which the latter two connected, stretching from the Tyrrhenian Sea across to the Adriatic Sea. Essentially, prior to our men ultimately breaching the third one of these obstacles, our allies' progress was hampered for months. Heavy offensives on the Winter Line and Anzio alone had seen us suffer 98,000 casualties while 60,000 Axis troops were killed, respectively.

However, due to the German defences above, our passing along the Cassino route would be impossible without first defeating the German troops on the mountain.

We (the Allies) started the first attack at Monte Cassino on 17 January 1944 with troops from the British Empire, America, and France valiantly fighting uphill against the strategic, German defences, which were extremely well integrated into the mountainside with a commanding view of the majority of activity occurring below. After sustaining huge losses, we were forced to pull back on 11 February.

Based on intelligence gathered, we were led to believe that the Germans were ensconced in the abbey for the purpose of using it as a military observation station and fortress despite an agreement dating back to 1933 classing it as neutral ground. This flagrant disregard of the latter incidentally still continued after the abbey was ruined. That had happened when we resolved to bomb it, which began the second stage of the offensive on 15 February 1944.

With the first and second battles having ended in failure for us, a month's careful planning took place before we launched a further offensive. For the third battle, it was eventually decided that the best option would be to launch twin attacks from the north using a mixture of heavy bombing (750 tons of 1,000-pound bombs with delayed action fuses that were dropped over a period lasting three and a half hours) and ground forces consisting of British, New Zealand, and Ghurka troops to allow a clear passage through the town of Cassino. Heavy losses were experienced on both sides mainly because the defences were seemingly impregnable. Rather frustratingly, the Germans held on to the abbey yet again.

Undeterred by having experienced three disastrous attempted assaults, the fourth attack, known as Operation Diadem and Operation Strangle started on the evening of 11 May 1944 with a mixture of yet more air strikes and a large contingent of troops made up principally of U.S. Fifth Army and British Eighth Army assisted by a corps of the British 4th and 8th Indian Infantry Divisions, 1st Canadian Armoured Brigade, Free French (including Moroccan Gourmiers) and the Polish corps. Besides its principal objective, Operation Diadem was planned to coordinate roughly with the invasion of Normandy so that German forces would be tied down in Italy and could not be redeployed to France.

The Polish corps broke through the German defences by 17 May, and on the following day, they captured the abbey at the top of Monte Cassino. Monte Cassino had, much to the relief of all of us, been conquered, and having finally broken the Winter line, we captured Rome on 4 June 1944. Even though the goal was now achieved, our success came at a cost with over 55,000 casualties compared to 20,000 losses on the German side. Back to Rusty, once the tale was out of his system, the magic of my mother's care and cooking coupled with the therapeutic value of the breathtaking lake and mountain scenery, he started to blot out the bad karma, a transformation that made us all happy. He survived the war and never forgot his stay with us.

Unlike the amazingly atmospheric and frighteningly fascinating first-hand account of Monte Cassino such that we felt we had really been there, which Rusty Gopel regaled us, including his liberating a bottle of Benedictine from a cellar in the town of Cassino, the story of what happened with the bombing of cities and industrial targets in Germany had to be pieced together from what we read in newspapers, heard on the radio or were selectively told by those who had experienced being on active service.

As mentioned earlier, the peace and tranquillity of the Lake District were rarely affected by enemy action, but elsewhere in

Europe, the activities of war were substantially increased. From 1942 onwards, with the appointment of Arthur "Bomber" Harris, a seasoned military man who was sometimes referred to as the "Butcher," there was an improvement in the accuracy and frequency using the large number of planes to bomb strategic industrial locations and cities at night time. His continued preference for area bombing rather than precision targeting remains controversial, partly because many senior allied air commanders thought it less effective and partly for the large number of civilian casualties and destruction the strategy caused. He justified his reasoning as follows:

> *"It has been decided that the primary objective of your operations should now be focused on the morale of the enemy civil population and in particular, of industrial workers."*

Harris prepared a list of 60 German cities he intended to destroy first:

> *"The aim is the destruction of German cities, the killing of German workers, and the disruption of civilised community life throughout Germany. It should be emphasised that the destruction of houses, public utilities, transport, and lives; the creation of a refugee problem on an unprecedented scale; and the breakdown of morale both at home and at the battle fronts by fear of extended and intensified bombing are accepted and intended aims of our bombing policy, they are not by-products of attempts to hit factories."*

However, it was not until January 1944 that Harris gained relative autonomy, having been promoted to the substantive rank of Air Marshal, and along with the British Chief of the Air Staff Charles Portal, he was convinced of the need for his vastly increased bomber force not only to carry on its programme of "precision bombing" but to also stop the random "area bombing" of cities until they were effectively completely obliterated being of the opinion that they would obtain "victory" within six months. Despite the amount of bombing rising from roughly 150,000 tons in 1943 to approximately 650,000 tons in 1943, it still did not bring about the supposed "Victory" within a mere six months, leaving the Second World War to be shortened by "D-Day."

Unbeknown to us in any way, the leaders of our allies reached a consensus that defeating the ogre of Nazi Germany could only be achieved by relieving the pressure on the Russians on the Eastern Front and establishing a vital second front in Northwest Europe. Then it was a case of where could be chosen for the best possible outcome as that was of great importance. Although Calais presented a quicker and shorter Channel crossing, it was, unfortunately, more heavily fortified than Normandy, which boasted ideal beaches for landing purposes and was still within reach by fighter aircraft.

Thus, the latter was chosen for the D-Day landings. Nevertheless, Calais was to play a major part in an elaborate diversionary scheme via agents circulating false reports and material in the vicinity accompanied by heavy bombing of the town. There were even fake armies, false radio traffic, and rubber tanks employed with the intention of distracting the Germans from the main area of conflict.

To manage the massive multi-national force bound for Normandy while the British General Bernard Montgomery was at the head of an army contingent of 160,000 soldiers, it was deemed necessary to create a Supreme Allied Command. Placed in charge of this body was the United States General Dwight D Eisenhower. Eisenhower not only had the gargantuan task of overseeing all air, land, and sea units involved, but also he was ultimately responsible for planning and supervising the invasion. To raise the morale of his men, he addressed them with the following speech.

"This operation is planned as a victory, and that's the way it's going to be. We're going down there, and we're throwing everything we have into it, and we're going to make it a success."

To ensure success initially, aerial reconnaissance provided scores of images showing the German defence with groups of Special Forces alighting on the Normandy coast to amass further useful information. Elsewhere the French resistance, along with others, not only busied themselves acquiring intelligence relating to the arrangement of German troops, but they also engaged in acts of sabotage against transport and communications networks. Meanwhile, the whole of southern England was seemingly covered by a continuous carpet of the masses of military equipment that had been brought together, comprising vehicles, tanks, supplies, and soldiers from several different nations. They underwent extensive training either in sections or individually in many different locations in the United Kingdom, one of which was very close to us.

It must have been around the early Spring of 1944. We were awakened at dawn by a lot of noise, activity, and clanking with associated shouting. My mother asked my sister Pat and me to get dressed quickly and go and investigate. At first, we approached tentatively, keeping a discreet distance but then we were spotted by a uniformed army officer who introduced himself as Canadian and asked for our help regarding the Lake frontage. There were lots of vehicles, equipment, and soldiers; It was buzzing with activity. Clearly, it was a military exercise to span the lake at this wide point with a pontoon bridge supported by barrels. What they wanted to know was whose was the jetty (next door's) and which was our frontage beach etc. which was more accessible. It was very exciting, and the Canadians were lovely guys. What we did not know was that this was practice for D Day on 6 June 1944.

Another lake exercise had tragic consequences. Again, it must have been a forerunner for D-Day as it involved landing craft. Men were sent out from Bowness into the Bay with shovels for oars but sadly wearing waterproof boots. The craft capsized, and six or seven men drowned because of their boots. The landing craft had floated off. Two or three evenings later, my sister and I out for a stroll went down to the water's edge a bit further along from our land, and half under an overhanging tree, we saw the landing craft (upside down) where it had been carried by the currents. We had to notify the Police, and it was very sad to think those men had lost their lives in such a terrible accident, and this was the craft in which they had cheerfully set out to their doom.

All too soon, it became readily apparent for those who did not perish in the rigorous practices that the gargantuan effort which was repeated was in aid of namely D-Day or Operation Overlord.

In spectacular fashion, it began on the afternoon of 5 June at 5.00pm when a flotilla of over five thousand ships set off from ports along our south coast for northwest France packed with troops and supplies that was fairly closely followed five hours later at 10.00pm by the first allied transport planes and gliders carrying the airborne invasion force. Their first tasks just after midnight on 6 June were to capture Pegasus Bridge and perform other necessary goals before the amphibious invasion, while American paratroopers swiftly snatched a town called Sainte-Mere-Eglise which was crucial to the campaign.

The campaign really got going not long after, at around 2.00am, with the first wave of fighters and allied bombers intent on weakening the German defences. Later on, they would serve up a relentless onslaught over the beach heads and strategic towns such as Caen before a combined Navy showered shells upon the enemy stationed along the Normandy coast.

To maintain secrecy particularly where communication was concerned, the beaches were given codenames: Utah and Omaha, which were naturally the designated disembarking points for the Americans, while British Forces landed at Gold, Sword, and Juno, assisted at the latter two by free French and Canadian troops respectively.

Of the total of one hundred and thirty thousand personnel involved in the battle, there were comparatively few casualties, some five thousand three hundred in all. Three thousand of these alone happened at Omaha and one thousand at Juno beaches due to a mixture of tough German defences in both instances as well as heavy seas in the second.

Despite such a resounding victory, much work still remained to be done to rid Europe of the tyranny of Nazi Germany, but a renewed impetus saw a rapid end to the conflict in less than a year or maybe looked at another way several months or perhaps even a couple of years were shaved off the Second World War.

Another fugitive from the battle was Bob Butler from the United States Air Force. He was a quiet, rather shy young man who arrived at our house soon after D-Day, where he had flown a glider full of troops to their planned destination and then had to find his way back to the allied lines because, of course, the glider could not take off again once it landed. He was smart in his generally acknowledged superior quality uniform, olive green jacket, and smooth pinkies – taupe-coloured trousers, but he was so badly affected by the D-Day experience that he could scarcely speak. Again, like Rusty, he slept for hours on end, recovering from complete exhaustion, but then he started to relax and enjoy his surroundings, the security of our family, and the peace of where we lived. He was a delightful young man who so appreciated the hospitality we offered him. He wrote me a message in my Autograph book, which I have always treasured, and later after the war, his father, Bill Butler, came to visit us at 'Melrose' near Manchester to express his gratitude.

How privileged I felt at nine years old in 1944 to have the good fortune to meet and spend some time with young men who were participants in events such as the Battle of Monte Cassino and D-Day, as well as having the stark realities of the Second World War brought home to me with the merciless bombardment of German cities which have all had a great significance and impact to the point that even so many years afterwards I still religiously commemorate their anniversary.

NEIGHBOURS

The next-door neighbours were not exactly as close by as it sounds being approximately a ten to fifteen-minute walk from Dick Intake, where we lived. In between was our cottage that was inhabited by the Flemings, who maintained the grounds of our house. We were just within the bounds of Westmorland (later Cumbria) and at the border with Lancashire. Nearby there was a huge half-hidden pill box to defend it if necessary. There were, of course, no road signs, as they had been removed in case of invasion. The house was of moderate size, but the garden which led down to the lake was beautifully terraced. There was a matching boathouse to the house, which was stuccoed. The owner was the widow of a Brazilian diamond millionaire, so the story went, and she lived with a companion, a Mrs Hewitt, who was the wife of the Captain of a Scottish Isles Steamer in peacetime whom my father had actually met. Their home port was Liverpool. Mrs Hewitt and her employer were two very pleasant ladies whose war effort was to offer hospitality to servicemen from the Commonwealth countries who naturally could not go home on leave. Mrs Boyes had two sons and a daughter but also nephews, one Canadian, Donny, one from South America maybe, John an officer in the British Army stationed at Salisbury Plain, and a third we never met who went missing in Burma, possibly a

Chindit. The Chindits (more commonly known as Long Range Penetration Groups) were the brainchild of Brigadier Orde Charles Wingate, and he amassed some nine to twelve thousand men drawn from the British and Indian Armies whose role was to cover vast distances on foot through extremely challenging terrain in Burma before making surprise attacks on Japanese troops, facilities and lines of communication despite often being underfed as well as weakened by diseases such as malaria and dysentery along with the extremely high casualties.

We were encouraged to use the telephone at their house as we did not have one of our own, and it was very helpful and useful. The procedure was that having been given permission by the owner, you rang the operator and asked for a transfer charge call to a given number. The Operator would reply that she would phone back when she had made the connection or say it was not possible. My sister waiting for the routine call, answered the phone when it rang, only to hear to her dismay that it was a man's voice; he assumed it was the owner of the house, ignored the attempted protests of my sister, and pressed on with the bad news that John had been cashiered from the Army having been caught with a woman in his barracks as it was said. It was a shocking breach of data protection. At the end of the sordid disclosure, my sister managed to reveal that it was his aunt who was next of kin, and then the story was retold to her. It was hugely embarrassing and, worst of all, regarded as a terrible disgrace in light of the sacrifices that were being made and the accepted standards of honourable behaviour. I used to wonder if he was allowed any self defence because he was magnetically attractive to women and had amazing charisma. Had he been set up? He was never reinstated, and we could not mention the incident to his aunt.

Sometime later, there arrived at our back door a completely dishevelled, heavily bearded, bedraggled, ragged young man asking to speak to my mother. We were stunned; it was John, who had been living rough in the woods next to our land for a while. He may have been helped by someone called Miss Harvey, who lived off a bumpy track in the same woods where he was sheltering, and she had a wooden hut attached to her house from which she sold eggs and a huge range of haberdasheries like hair ribbons, for example, which I needed for my plaits and knitting wool. I think it was possible to order things through her as well. When you arrived at the hut, you had to ring a bell, and then Miss Harvey would emerge from the depths of her house to see what you wanted. How this made a living for her, we did not know, but I think she may have been glad of the help of a big strong chap with military training in return for some food and warmth. Miss Harvey was intriguingly eccentric but very kind, and we sometimes thought we would walk down to see her without having an urgent need for some items.

My mother offered John the use of the bath, which he gratefully accepted, and found him clean clothes of my father's, and she and Lily made him some food before they talked. My mother, born in 1900, had been through the First World War, and after the Armistice, when she was 18 on 4th November 1918, there were hardly any males left alive of her age group in Bradford.

My father was born in 1902, and she was always very sensitive that he was younger, so she never revealed her age to anyone, a common situation with her female contemporaries. She told John he must not let a foolish mistake ruin his life and that he still had much to offer King and Country, and his self-respect must be preserved. He went off, and it was not long before he returned, having enlisted in the Merchant Navy as a stoker on an Atlantic convoy ship. We were thrilled even though the conditions and risks were pretty awesome. Aunty remained relentlessly unforgiving.

Some of the 'boys' who came to spend their leave next door I remember very clearly. Three were part of the crew of a Lancaster Bomber, and they served as Australian Air Force personnel but also flew for the R.A.F. The captain/pilot was called Jock, the Sparks radio officer was Bob, and the navigator was Charlie. They first met us, I think, when Mrs Boyes sent them to our house for eggs because my mother, wherever we lived, always kept hens and was an expert at it. She always maintained that you should never buy and eat eggs bought from a shop because their origin and history were unknown. She knew there could be a risk, but I do not think she knew about salmonella. Anyway Charlie, Bob, and Jock liked coming to our house and spending time with us. My mother, a Yorkshire woman, always had a plentiful supply of buns, Bakewell Tarts, etc., at the ready for these lads who were homesick and living a dangerous life with frequent bombing missions over Germany. I especially remember one visit at a weekend when my father was home. We were all together in the best room in the house, which contained our Grand Piano bought from the Wembley Exhibition. My father was a pianist good enough to have earned money playing in the YMCA in New York as an impoverished immigrant from the United Kingdom. Charlie, who was in his early twenties, dark and handsome, turned out to have a wonderful tenor voice, was engaged to a sweetheart in Australia whose favourite song which he sang was "I Dream of Jeanie with the Light Brown Hair."

My father said he would happily accompany him, and I have this spellbinding memory of the evening light, the view over the lake in the background, and Charlie's beautiful tenor voice delivering the words with passion and sincerity. It was incredibly emotional for all of us in different ways. The crew asked my father and mother if they would be their next of kin in Great Britain, to which they readily agreed. The three came again during the summer, and my parents suggested we arrange an outing on the lake with our big rowing boat and a picnic. It sounded exciting and was greeted with enthusiasm by the lads. The same weekend John, now a Merchant Navy stoker, came back on leave, and it was decided behind the scenes that he could not join the party without embarrassing questions being asked, so I was volunteered to go with him in Mrs Boyes's dinghy with our own picnic and keep well out of range if possible. I was flattered and thrilled that John was enthusiastic about the whole plan, and although I was only about eight or nine, he treated me as on the same level.

During the afternoon, we thought we heard the official boat party quite close and were slightly panicked, but there was an area of tall reeds into which boats had made channels. We slid into this strange world, knowing that their boat was too big to enter, and stayed absolutely stock-still, burying our faces in the cushions to stifle our laughter at the silly situation. This incident shows the awful snobbery which existed between the Merchant Navy and the Royal Navy. In 2020 some effort was made by the media to draw attention to the huge efforts put in by the Atlantic convoys and the debt owed to countless people who risked their lives in the former service. When we got back John told my mother he had had a lovely day, and I, of course, had too.

Later, he wrote a wonderful entry in my Autograph Book, and he survived the war, but I do not know what happened to him after that. Not long after the Big Picnic on the Lake, Jock contacted my father with the thrilling news that the number of successful bombing missions completed by his crew had merited an invitation to them all to go to Buckingham Palace to receive commendation medals from King George VI. Jock and the rest of the crew wanted my parents to be their English family as they were already nominated next of kin. My father and mother readily accepted, and after the ceremony at the Palace, he arranged a celebration luncheon at the Ambassadors Restaurant in London. On my parents' return to our house, they told us it had been a wonderful, joyous occasion. Bombing missions continued, then tragically, their Lancaster went missing over Dresden or Cologne, I am not sure which. My parents were notified by the War Office. Then one afternoon, on my return from school, I found all Jock's, Bob's, and Charlie's kitbags on the kitchen table with their possessions. It brought home to me how precarious survival was even for such strong, super young men as these. Even as recently as last year, I tried to find out what had happened to them from the Australian High Commission in London, but so far, I have not been successful.

On a much more cheerful note, one very memorable guest next door who appeared in the spring of 1944 was Ronald David Cooper. He already held the rank of Wing Commander in the Royal Australian Air Force and therefore was accompanied by his Batman, Lance Kelton, who came from Fremantle near Perth, Australia. We first encountered them when my sister, Pat, and I were cycling home from school one afternoon. On a long straight stretch of country lane, we could see two men with bicycles – one able to ride confidently (Lance) and the other unable to balance properly, falling off after very few turns of the pedals. As we virtually lived on our bicycles, we could not believe that an adult male was unable to cycle. Drawing level with them, of course, we could not help but stop. We had worked out that these two were probably from next door.

On introducing ourselves, there was a lot of laughter. David, as he preferred to be known, maintained that he knew he was going to marry my sister as soon as he saw her. Patricia, or Pat, as I called her, was extremely good-looking, a Grace Kelly/Veronica Lake type, but I think she was more glamorous than either of them. She had ash-blonde hair and cool features. The next day without bicycles, David and Lance gravitated to our house (I wonder why?) and introduced themselves to my mother and Lily. David was very charming with an extrovert personality, and he and Lance definitely lit up our lives. What we did not know was that this leave, and another one soon after, were forerunners to D-Day on 6 June, which was a carefully guarded secret.

We did not have any idea at all that such a momentous tide-turning event in the war was being planned intensively by Britain and our allies down to the last-minute detail. Even the early morning arrival of a contingent of Canadians (already described) to use our lake frontage to practise building a pontoon bridge from oil drums with a track strong enough to bear tanks did not make us suspect that this was more than a routine exercise.

The two chaps mentioned earlier were a part of a scarcely ever acknowledged Australian presence at the invasion. Their role was the responsibility for provisions and supplies to the Allied Forces, which they did so well that they were asked to take on a similar role in the allied invasion of Borneo. On D-Day, David was with RAF 2 Beach Squadron, and he always said only a few Australians took part. What that meant I have tried very hard to ascertain varying between approximately one thousand five hundred and three thousand – the latter according to the internet. Usually and rather shockingly, they seem not to have any mention at all. David said that he and his Company decided to spend the first night after landing in tents in a secluded French orchard. Lance went off foraging and returned bent double under the weight of a Bank Strong Room door he had found. His prize occasioned much derision from his mates, but he stood his ground, saying that he thought it would afford them some protection. How right he was because when they were asleep, a stray shell burst into the orchard and embedded itself in the Strong Room door without exploding, acknowledged by all to have saved many lives and prevented horrific injuries. For their superb achievement, David was subsequently awarded the Normandy medal by the French Government, so they were definitely there! I continue to try and obtain some recognition for them.

A CITY BREAK FROM THE LAKES

In summer 1944, my father must have decided it was relatively safe to venture to London for a week. He was very eager for me to see the Capital and what it had to offer, egged on by someone my sister and I referred to as 'Uncle' who was a theatre fanatic and expected that we would want to attend a matinee and evening performance every day of our stay! I hated being in the theatre in the afternoon because it gave me a bad headache which I could not describe or explain to anyone. However, we were all very excited about the adventure, and victory, a journey of about four and a half hours to London; it seemed very long to me, just short of nine years old.

We were going to stay at the Savoy Hotel, which was where my father regularly stayed in wartime, so much so he was allowed to go into the kitchens when he wanted, especially during air raids, as he would not go into public shelters at all. We arrived by London cab at the entrance off The Strand to be greeted by a doorman resplendent in his grey uniform, someone who recognised my father. We were taken to a family suite overlooking The Strand entrance and opposite the Savoy theatre with the Shell Mex Building tower in the background with its very distinctive clock. Dinner was served in our sitting room, and I was thrilled to find that my mother had discovered when placing the order that it was possible for me to have a Corn on the Cob, which I adored but was unable to have for a very long time because of the war. It was wonderful, and on my menu every night we were there. One evening we were going to see Ivor Novello's Musical "We'll gather Lilacs." My mother, along with hundreds of women of her generation, was besotted with Ivor and his music. We were engrossed in the production when the whole audience heard the menacing, terrifying throb of a Doodle Bug or V1 flying bomb over the theatre. Air Raid signs lit up red along the front of the stage. Characteristically the engine stopped, and everyone, including the cast, held their breath, waiting for a direct hit or an explosion elsewhere. Luckily it was the latter, and the performance continued uninterrupted and unruffled, but it was a stark reminder that we were still at war and at risk from an enemy far off.

Regarding the special relationship my father had with The Savoy Hotel because of his wartime stays and many years of loyalty after that, I heard only a year or two ago that a cousin Bill whom I never knew and had never met but with the same surname, McEvoy, booked a special wedding anniversary weekend at the hotel for himself and his wife. On arrival, Bill was greeted most warmly at the reception with, "It is a long time since we welcomed you here, and to show our pleasure, we have upgraded your suite to a riverside apartment." Bill trembling at the thought of the increased cost, managed to stammer, "You have made a mistake; I have never been here before. I think you may be confusing me with my cousin, Harry." The Savoy insisted on keeping the upgrade; I do not know whether Bill revealed to his wife that the rather grand apartment was not what he had originally booked but what is interesting is that my father, who was born in 1902, would have been at least one hundred and fifteen years old if he had still been alive, quite an elderly guest!

.

NEWS AND VICTORY DAYS

We normally heard the Radio, especially the bulletins at 1.00pm, 6.00pm, and 9.00pm, but because my father had strong connections with the press, we took the Westmorland Gazette, which is still going today, and three Sunday Newspapers, The News of the World, The Sunday People and Sunday Chronicle. When British troops found and repatriated Belsen Concentration Camp, my mother thought she had hidden the papers from me, but I knew where she had put them and secretly looked at the shocking and gruesome picture of a mountain of human remains. I was horrified but glad that I knew about it; I think it was on the front page of the News of the World, and I have never forgotten it. We also saw the news when we walked at least four miles to The Royalty Cinema between Bowness and Windermere to see a feature film; before that started, there was a Pathe Gazette newsreel (black and white, of course), but the news was usually about six months old, and the commentary was very loud and in upper-class English like Noel Coward spoke. One thing, however, that was really invaluable was that my father subscribed to Life Magazine, which I found super fascinating with its wonderful photography and realism. The documentation of the Second World War was fantastic, particularly in the Far East. We also had Time Magazine, but it was too sophisticated for me at such a young age. I just remember the covers which were famous. In our own world, Lily had magazines like Woman's World and Woman's Weekly. The former always featured a knitting pattern which she often made. She was a sensational and addictive knitter all her life. She taught me, and I got pretty hooked, too, especially on more complicated patterns like Fair Isle. Another welcome benefit of the United States joining the war was that we occasionally had American magazines which introduced us to the world of Hollywood and Hollywood Stars, a world of glamour and a level of culture above ours which seemed very attractive.

Probably the most important piece of news came on 8 May 1945. Prime Minister Winston Churchill made an announcement on the radio at 3pm that the war in Europe had come to an end, following Germany's surrender the day before. Captured by his mesmeric voice, it was something we listened to intently with our ears almost glued to the wireless.

"Yesterday morning at 2.41am at General Eisenhower's Headquarters, General Jodl, the representative of the German High Command, and Grand Admiral Doenitz the designated head of the German state, signed the act of unconditional surrender of all German land, sea, and air forces in Europe to the Allied Expeditionary Forces and simultaneously to the Soviet High Command. Hostilities will end one minute after midnight tonight, Tuesday 8th May. We may allow ourselves a brief period of rejoicing. Today is Victory in Europe Day. Tomorrow will also be Victory in Europe Day."

Victory in Europe or V.E. Day itself, I remember, brought an overwhelming sense of relief even though some people could not be in a celebratory mood because their lives had been irrevocably turned upside down by personal bereavement. The village was putting on some sort of evening celebration, so we decided we would walk into Bowness-on-Windermere to join what was going on. It was a fine night, and I remember that there was a big bonfire, some fireworks, and a lot of people on the Glebe, as it was called – a grassy area back from the lake.

Although we were celebrating a hard-earned success in one theatre of war, there were still thousands of troops embroiled in the conflict in the Far East, as we were reminded by the second half of Winston Churchill's speech.

"But let us not forget for a moment the toils and efforts that lie ahead. Japan, with all her treachery and greed, remains unsubdued. The injuries she has inflicted on Great Britain, the United States, and other countries and her detestable cruelties call for justice and retribution. We must now devote all our strength and resources to the completion of our tasks both at home and abroad. Advance Britannia, long live the cause of freedom. God Save The King."

Relentless and savage fighting brought about by the ruthless determination of the Japanese to gain supremacy brought about horrendous casualties not only among their civilian population and military personnel but also causing our forces to sustain heavy losses to the point that there was a need for something radical. Something radical did come fairly soon when events took a turn with the United Kingdom giving the United States the blessing to release two atomic bombs nicknamed Little Boy on Hiroshima and Fat Man on Nagasaki. Both cities as well as their inhabitants and workers were devastatingly vaporised with few exceptions to the point that a surrender of hostilities took place on 14th August 1945, with the following day dubbed Victory in Japan Day.

For the above occasion, we decided to have a huge bonfire in the field in front of the house and overlooking the lake. My sister and I and Fleming had piled up as much as we could burn when it was dark, and mum and Lily had made suitable food to eat. Not many years ago, my sister revealed to me that our Victory in Japan celebration was low key because our young postman, who had delivered and collected our mail before he was called up at eighteen years old, was killed just days before the Peace Treaty was signed by the Japanese. The news was kept from me, but everyone was very upset, my sister and Lily, in particular, because they had often chatted and joked together. He was just nineteen.

CHRISTMAS AT DICK INTAKE

Looking back, in spite of wartime with its food rationing and general anxiety, my parents managed to make every Christmas period a special and exciting time. My father was crazy about Christmas as far back as I can remember. I do not know if it was because he had spent time in America or if it harked back to his own childhood and preparations for the festive season in the grocer's shop my grandad ran in Bradford. Although it was a less privileged part of Bradford, it had many customers in the more affluent areas of the city and was very successful. My father used to recall that in the festive season, generous boxes of chocolate beautifully wrapped and beribboned used to be prepared as gifts for good customers. He remembered feeling envious and grudging as a nine-year-old having to accompany his father on the delivery rounds. But at one of the imposing, rather grand houses, the maid answered the door and behind her stood the most ravishing creature he had ever seen, a princess of eleven years old who stepped forward to receive the chocolates from him, which he did not begrudge any more – far from it, he had decided that when he grew up, he would marry this beautiful girl and so it was that she became my mother!

In our house at Christmas, we always had an enormous tree with long treasured decorations and ornaments, tinsel and lights, and a crib lighted too with all the traditional figures, which I loved to arrange in the straw. There was plenty of holly and mistletoe, too, without having to buy it. In spite of the rationing, we managed to have turkey every year with all the trimmings and mum's homemade Christmas puddings with plain white or whiskey sauce. We all wore our best clothes, and I remember one year my father had chosen for me a gorgeous party dress, white embroidered with the lily of the valley and a pale green sash. It came from Debenham and Freebody's in London in a beautiful box.

Pantomime was a part of Christmas we could not miss despite the war and living a journey of two and a half hours away from Manchester by train. So sometime after school had broken up, we used to go to Windermere Station via a car sent out from Bowness to catch the train to Manchester Exchange. My mother had made sure that we were warmly and smartly dressed in our Jaeger coats with brown velour hats, brown lace-up shoes, and socks not white but ecru because, according to her, white showed up any steam train smuts. We had to wear gloves as well, though. When I was five and six, my sister and I had matching beaver muffs to keep our hands warm and pixie beaver hats to match. I remember it was wonderfully soft, quite silky fur.

On arrival at our destination, we either went to Kendal Milnes, the big famous department store in Deansgate so that mum could visit the millinery department and consult the manager, Miss Beaver, about the latest models she could try on and usually buy or go straight to the Midland Hotel for lunch prior to the matinee performance of the Pantomime at the Palace Theatre. The entrance to the Midland was protected by a huge concrete screen against blast and reinforced with sandbags. The restaurant's menu was very restricted with what seems now bizarre choices like Palethorpes Sausages, mashed potatoes, and some vegetables. My fear was that I would not always be able to finish all the food on my plate, as I have said before.

Going to the theatre in the afternoon was exciting but always gave me a headache which I did not know how to describe to anyone. Performances were of a high standard and normally funny and enjoyable despite the head hurting so much. Perhaps it was because people smoked in the auditorium. I remember one December, I could hardly wait to get on the train home. I flopped in the carriage seat just as it was announced that there was a twenty-minute delay. I fell soundly asleep against my mother's shoulder and awoke much later, hoping we were nearly home, only to discover that the train had not been allowed to leave the station at all because, for over an hour, a raid was in progress and the fire and the sparks from the engine might have given away the position of the train, the station, etc., as a possible target. It was very alarming, and we got home really late. Lily had been worried, of course, but no contact was possible like it would be now with a mobile phone.

Given the very limited communication which was available in the 1940s, it was impossible to know or see what was available in book form, so we had to make an expedition to the bookshop which was in Windermere (now W.H.Smith), usually at Christmas or after a birthday which meant there were book tokens to be exchanged probably for values of five shillings, ten shillings or twenty-one shillings which you will find laughable. I think my first visit to the bookshop was in 1941, and my parents bought us family bibles. Mine is bound in brown leather and contains sepia pictures of sites in the Holy Land. This Bible has been close to me all my life which is, I am sure, what my parents wanted for my sister and me when they purchased those Bibles so long ago.

Christmas 1945 was especially poignant. It was an enormous relief to be no longer under threat from two enemies, but, of course, sadly, it meant that our lives were going to change drastically early in January 1946.

My father was desperately ill and facing major surgery for the removal of a kidney, and my mother must have been worried out of her mind, but as someone born in 1900 like the Queen Mother, she never showed any lack of resolve. Perhaps experiences of two world wars with the nationally devastating Great Depression in between had prepared her for anything.

As children, we were facing the unknown. People had come over Christmas as always, but it was in the nature of farewells, so not very cheering. Saying goodbye to Oakburn and my friends here had been tough, though I would not miss the lunches, and then there was the environment we were accustomed to, with open spaces, the glorious scenery with the lake and mountains. Leaving such idyllic beauty along with Dick Intake, Fleming, and Mrs Fleming was going to be awful, and my beloved cats except for Ginger. Ginger was coming with us. I remember the long car journey well because as we did not have a cat basket at all in those days, he slept on my lap the whole way, purring contentedly. Once we finally arrived home which was in a partially built-up area of Stockport on the main A6 road bustling as it did with traffic, including trams and buses, every time my sister and I caught sight of Ginger, he made us reminisce about our adventure in the Lake District.

Printed in Great Britain
by Amazon

35172554R00078